Nuffield Trust Series No.16

Auditing the Auditors

Audit in the National Health Service

Patricia Day
Rudolf Klein

Foreword by
John Wyn Owen

LONDON: The Stationery Office

The Nuffield Trust

FOR RESEARCH AND POLICY
STUDIES IN HEALTH SERVICES

Applications for reproductions should be made in writing to The Stationery Office Limited, St Crispins, Duke Street, Norwich NR3 1PD
The information contained in this publication is believed to be correct at the time of manufacture. Whilst care has been taken to ensure that the information is accurate, the publisher can accept no responsibility for any errors or ommissions or for changes to the details given.

A CIP catalogue record for this book is available from the British Library.
A Library of Congress CIP catalogue record has been applied for.

First published 2001

ISBN 0 11 702752 9

Typeset by Graphics Matter Limited, Lowestoft, Suffolk

Printed in the United Kingdom by The Stationery Office
TJ 004234 C7 8/01 19585

About the authors

Patricia Day is Senior Research Fellow at the University of Bath.

Rudolf Klein is Emeritus Professor of Social Policy, University of Bath, and Visiting Professor at the London School of Economics and at the London School of Hygiene and Tropical Medicine.

They have collaborated on a series of studies of the machinery of accountability and regulation in the public sector. Their publications include: Accountabilities: five public services in 1987 and How organisations measure success: the use of performance indicators in government (with Neil Carter) in 1992.

FOREWORD

In Michael Power's book, *The Audit Society. Rituals of Verification* [1] he outlines the explosion of auditing activity in the United Kingdom and North America and he asks: Why has this happened? What does it mean when a society invests so heavily in an industry of checking and when more and more individuals find themselves subject to formal scrutiny? Power argues that the use of auditing has its roots in political demands for accountability and control. He questions the manner in which auditors produce assurance and accountability, suggests the possibility that auditors may impose their own values and argues that audits can have unintended and dysfunctional consequences for the audited organisation. Power queries whether the fashion for auditing signifies a distinctive phase in the development of advanced economic systems as they grapple with production risks, erosion of social trust, fiscal crisis and the need for control: all under the umbrella of accountability.

These are very much the questions that I have pondered in my various posts as an Accounting Officer within the UK Civil Service; as Director of the NHS in Wales when the Audit Commission's remit was extended to health services with the Thatcher Reforms; as the Chairman of a Health Authority; and as part of the Chief Executive Service of the State Health Department in New South Wales, Australia. Further, the Auditor-General's office in New South Wales adopted the Audit Commission's approach to value-for-money auditing and even had an exchange of staff with the UK Audit Commission.

In 1998 the Trustees awarded a grant to Patricia Day and Rudolf Klein to undertake a research project "Auditing the NHS. The role of the Audit Commission". Over the past decade there has been increasing emphasis on accountability in the NHS, along the lines that Power identifies, with the aim of improving performance by making activities more visible so as to promote economy, effectiveness and efficiency in the use of resources. The Day and Klein study was designed to examine the work of the Audit Commission in the wider context of accountability in the NHS. The Audit Commission is only one of a number of bodies – both old and new – charged with reporting on the NHS but it has developed a distinctive style, both carrying out national studies and auditing the performance of local NHS bodies. It also has experience of collaboration with other inspectorates. The aim of the study was therefore to examine both its national and local activities and the impact of its work on the NHS, to identify the lessons to be drawn from its experience and expertise in defining and assessing the various dimensions of performance – fiscal, organisational and managerial. The study in particular examines the relationship of the Audit Commission's activities with those of the National Audit Office and the new Commission for Health Improvement.

In respect of one of the most important questions about the Audit Commission - its impact on the NHS – Day and Klein conclude that it is difficult and probably impossible to answer. The strength of the Audit Commission lies in its ability to follow up national studies through local auditors. Its weakness is that there is no natural forum for those national studies and therefore no national machinery for following up its recommendations at the level of national policy. This is the price the Commission pays for its independence of government.

Day and Klein, as a result of their analysis, pose that there is an alternative approach to evaluating the performance of audit institutions and, instead of asking for evidence of change in the NHS as a result of their activities, we could start from the presumption that they should be judged in terms of their contribution to strengthening public accountability, and ask for evidence about their effectiveness in making the activities of publicly-funded services and programmes transparent as well as meshing with the institutional machinery of accountability. This would require making management letters more explicit, more comprehensive and more accessible. Now with the opportunity for local authorities to scrutinise the activities of the NHS, this provides an opportunity to establish a link between the Audit Commission and the political institutions and the local community. Similarly at the national level, the Audit Commission's work could support the work of the Health Committee of the House of Commons – strengthening the Committee as well as giving the Commission a national forum which it now lacks. These proposals are worthy of deliberation.

John Wyn Owen CB
London: March 2001

EXECUTIVE SUMMARY

- Over the past decade a complex machinery of accountability has developed in the National Health Service as successive generations of politicians have created new institutions of audit, review and inspection. This study concentrates on the role of the Audit Commission, whose activities are more pervasive in the NHS than that of any of the other bodies, and examines its role in the crowded arena in which it operates. In particular, it examines the relationship of its activities with those of the venerable National Audit Office and the new Commission for Health Improvement.

- The Audit Commission, through its local auditors, is responsible for inspecting the books and activities of all NHS bodies. The work of the auditors is split 70% to 30% between the annual financial audit and Value for Money (VFM) or performance audit. The former extends beyond ensuring probity and regularity to examining the internal control capacity of the audited bodies and their ability to identify risks. The importance of this activity cannot be exaggerated. But this study concentrates on the Commission's VFM activities - concerned with economy, efficiency and effectiveness (the three Es) in the use of resources - since these are more contentious in the NHS.

- Local VFM audits are preceded by national studies produced centrally by the Commission. These are based on extensive field work in the NHS and informed by the advice of expert bodies. They provide the agenda for local VFM studies and inputs for training local auditors, an activity in which the Commission invests much effort. The main focus of these studies has been on services for patients. Studies of governance issues (like fraud prevention) and household matters (like waste management) have been very much in the minority.

- The national studies have directed a powerful searchlight on the activities of the service, providing a unique and unflattering portrait of the NHS. They have illuminated, among other things, the information poverty of the service, the seemingly haphazard patterns of staff deployment and the lack of explicit and coherent policies in trusts. If the NHS has been perceived as starved of resources it is therefore in part at least because of the way those resources have been used: the fact that the Audit Commission's studies have always been able to find exemplars of good practice suggests that the capacity to deliver good quality services, holding budgetary constraints constant, is unequally distributed. Improving that capacity may therefore be as important as increasing resources.

- In carrying out their task auditors face a major challenge: how to define the criteria for assessing the performance of the service or organisation being audited. Ready made templates for service organisation are rarely available. An analysis of the process of producing two national studies (diabetes services; critical care) and training local auditors to carry them into the field, led to the conclusion that the auditor's craft depends on skill in negotiating the elusive and ambiguous meaning of "performance" and on diplomacy in treading the delicate path between the traditional audit, preoccupation with the three Es and professional practice. Auditors have to challenge the organisation of clinical services without directly challenging clinical practice.

- In assessing performance, auditors also use three sets of all-purpose tools which can be applied irrespective of the topic being examined. First, they use "rational actor" model of decision making. If an organisation lacks data about how its resources are distributed, if it does not routinely monitor how those resources are being used and if it lacks information about outcomes, then there is a prima facie case for considering that resources are not being managed either efficiently or effectively.

Second, comparative data is used to question the performance of the audited body: the guiding assumption is that variations in themselves demonstrate that there is scope for those at the bottom of any distribution to improve their performance. Third, and increasingly, the consumer perspective is invoked in assessing the quality of services.

- The most important question about the Audit Commission – its impact on the NHS – is difficult, and probably impossible, to answer. The Audit Commission, in sharp contrast to the National Audit Office (NAO), sees its primary role as being to improve the efficiency and effectiveness of services rather than saving money. But improvements in service organisation and delivery in the NHS are the products of many factors and it is impossible to isolate the contribution of the Commission and local auditors in bringing it about. The diplomatic skill and professional know-how of local auditors are necessary but far from sufficient conditions for opening the doors to change – but will not, in themselves, ensure that managers and clinicians actually walk through that door.

- Interviews with a range of managers suggest, however, that the Audit Commission has made a positive impact on the service in terms of the impressions made on those working in the NHS. The national studies get a high rating. Views on local audits are more mixed. Financial audit is held in high regard and, in turn, has contributed to an improvement in NHS financial systems; VFM audit is rather less well respected. Much depends on the quality of the local auditors. Similarly, much depends on whether audit topics are seen as relevant to local concerns. In both respects, however, recent improvements in audit performance are reported.

- The strength of the Audit Commission lies in its ability to follow up national studies through local auditors. Its weakness is that there is no natural forum for those national studies and therefore no machinery for following up its recommendations at the level of national policy, even though many of these call for changes in strategy or practice by the NHS Executive. This is the price the Commission pays for its independence of government.

- The strengths and weaknesses of the prestigious National Audit Office provide a mirror image. Its reports go to, and are followed up by, the powerful Public Accounts Committee of the House of Commons. There is therefore a strong incentive for Whitehall to pay heed. Conversely, however, it has no instruments for the diffusion of its recommendations at the periphery.

- As long as the prime audience of the Audit Commission remains those engaged in service delivery at the periphery, while that of NAO remains the world of policy makers at the centre, this assymetry does not matter. And, for most of the time the two audit organisations have successfully managed to differentiate their style and products even when they have investigated the same subject areas in the NHS. But there are now signs not so much of duplication as of convergence: some recent NAO reports, for example, the report on hospital acquired infections, have addressed advice directly to trusts and clinicians. Generally NAO's VFM work has shifted from a preoccupation with systems of control in the 1980s – when it represented 80% of the work done - to an emphasis on substantive issues in the 1990s.

- Convergence, in this and other respects, does not necessarily imply imitation. It reflects the fact that audit as an art form adapts to wider changes in government and society. All audit bodies and inspectorates are responding to the government's agenda for modernising the public sector. In particular, they are responding to the emphasis on joined-up government and service delivery. The Audit Commission is particularly well placed to exploit this opportunity, since its remit covers local government and it has experience of developing, with the Department of Health's Social Services Inspectorate, a system of joint reviews of social services departments.

- However, the emphasis on joined-up, co-ordinated service delivery represents a challenge, as well as an opportunity, for audit bodies; this is how to co-ordinate their own activities efficiently and effectively. The problem is compounded by the arrival of the Commission for Health Improvement (CHI) on the scene. Although its concern is with clinical governance and the quality of services, there is clearly a risk of overlap or duplication with the Audit Commission's concern with fiscal governance and the 3 Es: logically, it is impossible to examine efficiency and effectiveness without also looking at quality (can a low quality service be effective?).

- At present, the risk of a collision between the two Commissions is theoretical only. They have established mechanisms for co-ordinating their activities, and CHI is leaning on the resources of the Audit Commission. Similarly, the Audit Commission and NAO have established procedures for discussing their programmes. However, it is important to recognise that audit institutions, like all other organisations, have an interest in self-preservation, if not in expanding their turf. There is a case, therefore, for quinquennial reviews – across the board – of the activities of the various auditors and inspectors in the NHS to monitor both the degree of co-ordination between them and the load they impose on the service.

- The Audit Commission is adapting its strategy to a changed environment. It is responding to criticism in the NHS (see above) by offering a larger range of VFM studies à la carte, rather than a limited and fixed menu as in the past: at the same time the Commission's agenda will be integrated more closely with the NHS's priorities. It is also, like NAO and CHI, putting even more emphasis on incorporating a consumer perspective in assessing performance. Given that the NHS is also multiplying its investment in eliciting consumer views, this may carry a long-term risk of introducing a new iatrogenic complaint in the NHS: survey fatigue. There would seem to be a case, in the interests of economy and efficiency, for the various parties to agree on a standard model for consulting users and citizens so that a single set of data would be more acceptable to all of them.

• The Audit Commission is also proposing to invest in research to establish the characteristics of successful VFM reviews: success being defined in terms of bringing about change in the NHS. This raises a more general worry. Everyone in the field – the Commission, NAO and CHI – now appear to be competing to measure their effectiveness in these terms. But this would seem to be stretching the function of audit and inspection to breaking point by drawing it into the sphere of change engineering and management consultancy, so creating role confusion.

• There is an alternative approach to evaluating the performance of audit institutions, starting from the presumption that they should be judged in terms of their contribution to strengthening public accountability. Instead of asking for evidence of change in the NHS as a result of their activities, we could be asking for evidence about their effectiveness in making the activities of publicly funded services and programmes transparent as well as meshing with the institutional machinery of accountability.

• In the case of the Audit Commission this would suggest a rather different set of policy concerns and options from those prompted by the change-management perspective. At present the final reports of local auditors – the management letters – tend to be diplomatically phrased. They are addressed to the client, i.e. the body being audited, not to the public, though they are publicly available. If the Audit Commission's performance is to be judged in terms of giving transparency to the NHS, there is a case for making management letters more explicit, more comprehensive and more accessible. The model for so doing already exists: the reports of the Joint Review Teams.

- The argument for moving in this direction is reinforced by the Government's decision, in the NHS Plan, to allow local authorities to scrutinise the activities of the NHS in their area. This offers an opportunity to establish a link between the Audit Commission and the political institutions of the local community: the reports of local auditors could, if beefed up, be a significant input into this new, if weak, line of accountability. Similarly, at the national level, the Audit Commission's work could support the inquiries of the Health Committee of the House of Commons. This would have a double advantage. It would strengthen the Committee. And it would give the Commission a national forum in which to display its work.

ACKNOWLEDGEMENTS

This study could not have been carried out without the co-operation of the various bodies whose activities are analysed in the text. They have (with a single exception noted in the text) been exceptionally helpful, candid and very free with their information. They have given us access to much material, unpublished as well as published. And they have been generous of their time: a great many busy people freed space in their diaries for interviews and also allowed us to tag along to various training and study sessions in the field without complaining about us getting in the way of their work. The interviews and observations were carried out on a non-attributable basis. We therefore cannot thank the individuals concerned by name but would like to record our gratitude to our anonymous helpers.

As the principal focus of our study, the Audit Commission also bore the brunt of our inquiry. So particular thanks go to its staff. Their patience was remarkable, all the more so since in a fast changing situation we frequently had to ask for repeat interviews and discussions in order to keep up with events.

Responsibility for the analysis of the activities of the various audit bodies, and the conclusions drawn, lies entirely with the authors. Not the least impressive part of the co-operation given was that no conditions were imposed.

Lastly, our thanks go to John Wyn Owen and Max Lehmann at the Nuffield Trust. Not only did they fund the study. But they suffered patiently (and in silence) when we fell behind schedule in delivering this text.

September 2000
Patricia Day and Rudolf Klein

INTRODUCTION

Over the past decades increasing emphasis has been put on accountability in the National Health Service, as part of a larger transformation in the way public services are organised and managed (1). New institutions have been created to monitor, and give visibility to, the activities of the NHS. In 1990 the NHS and Community Care Act extended the brief of the Audit Commission from local government to the NHS, with responsibility not only for checking the accounts but with promoting economy, efficiency and effectiveness. In addition, it set up the Clinical Standards Advisory Group to review standards of clinical care and access for patients. In 1999 the Health Act created the Commission for Health Improvement to scrutinise the NHS's quality of service performance, replacing the Advisory Group. The new institutions were additions to the existing architecture of accountability. The remit of the National Audit Office, Parliament's instrument for scrutinising the way in which public resources are used, continues to cover the NHS. At the same time the managerial hierarchy of control, stretching from the Department of Health to the periphery, has been streamlined and strengthened. Performance indicators have proliferated.

The result is a distinctly Gothic machinery of accountability, as successive generations of politicians have added new buttresses and spires to the old building. The relationship of the different auditors to each other is not clear. How distinctive are their roles? Is there a risk of overlap or competition, and a consequent danger of over-audit? Nor is it clear how far audit should be seen as an instrument for calling the government to account for its stewardship of the NHS, as distinct from being an instrument for improving the performance of the NHS and strengthening the centre's ability to control what is happening at the periphery. Who are the audiences for audit? Is the aim to inform the public or to assist management? The puzzles do not stop there. The phrase "monitoring the performance of the NHS" trips off the tongue easily enough. But who defines the "performance" that is being monitored and how? And can a structure of accountability and audit designed to check the way in which resources are used by individual government departments or programmes be adapted to fit in with New Labour's agenda for modernising government with its emphasis on working across departments and programmes?

These are some of the questions which shape this study of the Audit Commission: a focus justified by the fact that its activities are more pervasive in the NHS than those of any of the other bodies. The first section of this report analyses the work, strategies and methodologies of the Commission, what its reports tell us about the NHS and how it is perceived by the NHS. The second section then examines the roles of other audit agencies, in particular that of the NAO. The final part then returns to the more general issue of the structure of audit and accountability in the NHS. In all this we use the term "audit" in a loose, non-technical way. Our reason for doing so is that while the traditional definition of audit - as the verification of the accounts and the assurance of regularity and probity in the use of resources (2) - captures one essential dimension of the activity, it is no longer an adequate description of what goes on. As audit has moved out from its core role, and widened its scope to include Value-for-Money (VFM) studies, so it has become increasingly difficult to maintain a sharp distinction between the activities of auditors, inspectors and consultants. Nor is this a definitional problem only. As auditors have widened the scope of their activities, so a new set of problems has arisen . While the authority or legitimacy of accountants to determine what counts as good performance in managing finances is rarely challenged - though even this is more art than science (3) - auditors can claim no special expertise when they examine other dimensions of organisational activity. Indeed in doing so, they pose a challenge to the expertise of others: for example, in the case of the NHS, that of doctors and nurses. As the boundaries of audit have expanded, so have the opportunities for dispute and friction: a theme which emerges strongly from the experience of the Audit Commission.

PART 1 - THE AUDIT COMMISSION

1.1 Setting the scene

The Audit Commission has a number of distinctive features. First, it is a non-departmental public body with its own independent board. The Commissioners are appointed by the Secretaries of State for the Environment, Transport and the Regions, for Health and for Wales. The membership changes over time, but invariably includes people with experience - whether as former civil servants, ex-presidents of Royal Colleges, managers or trust chairs - of the NHS. The Commission sees itself, in the words of a former chairman (4), as "a fearless independent commentator, with the authority and the ability to challenge received wisdom and the integrity that comes from being immune to political manipulation". It may criticise not only the services under review but also government policies. In contrast, as we shall see in Part 11, the National Audit Office is the instrument of Parliament and is specifically barred from questioning policy while the Commission for Health Improvement is very much the instrument of the Secretary of State for Health. Second, only the Audit Commission has a network of local auditors charged with annually verifying the accounts, reviewing the fiscal performance and selectively examining the activities of all health authorities, Trusts and Primary Care Groups (as well, of course, as local authorities).

The Commission appoints local auditors on a rotating basis. These are drawn either from the Commission's own "arm's length agency", District Audit, which carries out 71% of the work (4), or from private accountancy firms: the Treasury has pressed for a 50/50 public/private split, but the Commission has resisted this at least partly because of the difficulty of attracting private firms for whom NHS audit is a high risk, low volume and low return business, though it brings kudos and credibility. The Commission is responsible for determining the level of fees, setting the audit standards and reviewing the quality of the audits carried out. Finally the Commission is entirely self-financed, receiving no government grant or subsidy. Its income comes almost wholly from the audit fees charged.

The work of the auditors is, as already indicated, divided between traditional probity and regularity audit and VFM studies, with 70% of their time being devoted to the former and 30% to the latter. While the function of verifying the accounts of the audited bodies - i.e. establishing whether they give a true picture of their financial state - is traditional, the methods used have changed and continue to do so. In line with general developments in audit (3) the emphasis has switched to establishing whether the internal control systems of the bodies being audited are adequate and, in particular, whether sufficient attention has been paid to systematically identifying risks. Importantly, too, auditors are responsible for identifying - and reporting privately to the Secretary of State - instances of expenditure incurred unlawfully or likely to cause a loss or deficiency. In 1996, 16 such cases were reported; in 1997, the figure was 10 (6). The subjects of these reports included staff relocation and removal expenses, payments made to staff on leaving the NHS and the use of GP fundholders' savings to buy property. Auditors may also issue "public interest" reports, where they feel an issue is important enough to demand attention: in these cases, the report must be considered at a public meeting by the body concerned. These are rare, dribbling out at the rate of one or two a year. Normally, however, local auditors report only to the body being audited, which is seen as the client for the work, and put any reservations they may have in the management letter that marks the end of each year's exercise: a letter addressed to the board concerned which, however, is now generally made available to the public.

All this is much more than a neutral, technical exercise, it must be stressed. Much judgement is involved. In particular, establishing whether the accounts give a true picture of the financial standing of a health authority or trust may be far from simple. If, for example, such an authority or trust is heading for a deficit - a common enough situation - the auditor has to form a judgement as to whether the plans for making economies are realistic and whether the executives concerned have the ability to achieve them. Over-optimistic assumptions about the scope for making savings often explain financial disasters (7). The auditors therefore have to assess not only the figures in the balance sheet but also the managerial capacity of the organisation concerned when giving their verdict.

The procedures for carrying out VFM audits are somewhat different. While the financial audit is an automatic, annual process, VFM studies are carried out selectively. The Audit Commission regularly carries out national studies on a range of topics (see below). These then become the menu of local audit offered to the audited bodies. In each case, there is intensive training for the auditors and a handbook is prepared to guide them. As in the case of financial audit, there is a process of negotiation to determine how much time should be spent by the auditors in carrying out their task in any individual health authority or trust: an important consideration for those being audited, since time translates into money. Unlike financial audit, those carrying out the work are not necessarily accountants by original trade: the recruitment net for VFM auditors has been spread more widely and the staff now includes nurses, managers and others with experience of working in the NHS as well as arts and sciences graduates seeking audit training.

In addition, the Audit Commission works with the Department of Health's Social Services Inspectorate in reviewing the performance of local authority social service departments (8). These inspections are carried out by joint teams, bringing together the expertise of Commission staff and the professional perspective of the SSI. And although local authority services fall outside the scope of this study, we shall briefly examine this experiment in joined-up-inspection - given both the inter-dependence of the NHS and social services and the growing emphasis being put on cross-boundary work (see section 2.2).

So much, then, for the overall picture. Many of the details will be filled in and amplified in the sections that follow. These will analyse particular aspects of the Audit Commission's work. In doing so the emphasis will be on the Commission's VFM work. This is not because we regard financial audit as being of lesser importance: indeed, to anticipate our conclusions, we believe this to be the Commission's most valuable function. However, VFM audit is both more visible and more contentious. The Commission's national studies attract much media attention and the local VFM work sparks off most criticism. It is also in this area that there is most risk of duplication with other inspectorial or audit bodies. Hence while the focus of this study on VFM work may appear disproportionate in terms of the balance of work carried out by the Commission, it accurately reflects the fact that it is this aspect of its activities which is most prominent in the public eye.

1.2 The scope of national VFM studies

Since acquiring responsibility for the NHS, the Audit Commission has issued national reports on a wide range of topics. Table 1 sets these out under three headings. The first heading covers reports dealing with the management, financial and organisational, and governance of NHS authorities and trusts. The second covers reports dealing with patient care issues, i.e. the way in which services are organised and staffed in order to deliver services which, directly or indirectly, affect the care received by patients.

The third covers reports which deal with the way in which services, which bear only indirectly on patient care but are important in resource terms are managed. The list does not cover all the outputs of the Commission. We have not included the series of Management Papers issued by the Commission - dealing with such topics as the role of non-executive directors. And at least one national report - a study of the performance of fundholders - has been excluded because it does not fit into our categories. The table lists the reports by the topic covered rather than the titles: the Commission is much given to devising catchy titles for reports, which do not necessarily convey the subject matter.

One message is clear from Table 1. The main focus of Audit Commission's national VFM studies, which provide the themes for local auditors, is on services for patients. It is these studies which have dominated its activities. Its approach and style in doing so will become clear below when we look at some of the reports in more detail and in section 1.4 where we examine the Commission's methodology and the way in which it constructs its notion of what "good performance" means: i.e. the criteria against which health authorities and trusts are to be assessed. In doing so, as we shall see, it treads a delicate path between concentrating on the organisational management of services and challenging professional practice.

First, though, there is the question of how the Commission chooses the topics for study. No simple answer is possible. From time to time the Commission trawls the NHS for suggestions to see what the customers want. Over the years questionnaires have been sent out to Chief Executives, Directors of Finance, Directors of Nursing, Medical Directors and Directors of Public Health. Focus groups have also been used. But such consultation exercises rarely, if ever, produce a clear-cut agenda. On the one hand, response rates to surveys tend to be low, suggesting a certain lack of interest in the Commission's activities among people working in

Table 1 Topics covered by Audit Commission reports

1. Governance/ Management	2. Patient Care Issues	3. Household Matters
The role of District Health Authorities	Day Surgery	Supplies management
The role of Family Health Authorities	Nursing Management Systems	Management of hospital waste
Ensuring probity, preventing fraud	Community Care	
An audit agenda for providers	The use of medical beds in acute hospitals	
Management costs	Pathology services	
Management of staff turnover	Hospital services for children	
	Better prescribing in general practice	
	Information management in acute hospitals	
	Information management in Community Trusts	
	Hospital medical records	
	The work of hospital doctors	
	Co-ordinating care for elderly patients with hip fracture	
	Managing radiology services	
	Commissioning services for coronary heart disease	
	Hospital medical staffing	
	A & E services	
	Anaesthesia and pain relief services	
	Care services for older people	
	Emergency ambulance services	

the NHS. On the other hand, the responses that do come back usually show a lack of agreement about what the Commission should be doing. In one such exercise, carried out in 1997, the response rate was 39% and only 13 topics were chosen by more than five people out of the 348 who replied (9). In short, when the customers are asked, there is cacophony rather than consensus (which doesn't stop the customers complaining, as we shall see, about the lack of fit between the Commission's activities and their own needs).

Given that there is a constant flow of suggestions from other sources as well, producing an excess of potential topics, much depends on the Commission's own internal procedures for deciding what to pursue. These procedures, and the criteria used, are in the process of change (see Part 3). But the essential elements are preliminary studies to identify a short list of candidates which then are sifted by the managerial hierarchy of the Commission for approval by a Panel of the Commission's members. When deciding on a programme of work, a number of criteria are used. First, the programme should offer something to everyone: acute trusts, community trusts and so on. Second, there is the "materiality" test: i.e. that the topic area should be one where considerable sums of money are being spent. Third, the inquiry should offer prospects of savings (though in practice, as we shall see, many are likely to make a case for more money - as well as more efficient ways of spending it). Fourth, that the topic should offer an opportunity to look at services from the users' point of view. Fifth, the national study should be "doable": an elusive but crucial concept further explored in the next section on methodology. More generally the Commission aims over time to cover all the NHS's activities (providing they pass the "materiality" test) and to build on the findings of earlier reports. So much for the scope of the Commission's activities and the processes for determining its programme of work. What of the contents of the national studies? Boxes 1-3 give brief, schematic summaries of a sample of reports. In what follows, however, we will not discuss individual reports in detail. Instead we propose to concentrate on analysing what is common to them - the themes running through them - in order to identify what they tell us both about the Commission's own approach to VFM audit and about the state of the NHS.

Box 1 Governance/Management issues

Trusting in the Future: Towards an Audit Agenda for NHS Providers (1994)

1. Aim: to clarify duties of trust boards and key management issues facing chief executives.

2. Methodology: Ten site visits by Audit Commission, a survey of 400 staff in those units, NHS statistics and academic research findings. An advisory group of nine (predominantly NHS managers, with a sprinkling of academics).

3. Target audience: Executive and non-executive Board members.

4. Findings: Wide variations between trusts in the number and structure of clinical directorates, in productivity of clinical staff and in sickness absence and staff turnover; lack of management information; failure to keep staff informed.

5. Recommendations: For boards, the message is that they must give a clear direction; ensure a system of individual accountability and control; develop a programme of performance review based on suitable performance indicators. For managers, the message is that they must have a programme of precise performance targets, covering quality standards as well as activity levels; that they must invest more in communication and consultation with staff and improve the availability of information.

Protecting the Public Purse: Ensuring probity in the NHS (1994)

1. Aim: to strengthen existing arrangements for preventing fraud and corruption.

2. Methodology: A survey of all directors of finance (70% response rate); a review of all management letters produced by auditors in previous year; visits to 17 NHS bodies and interviews with 586 people. An advisory group of 18 (NHS finance experts, auditors and policemen).

3. Target audience: NHS Executive, managers and non-executive members of NHS boards.

4. Findings: Over previous three years, health authorities and trusts reported 960 known cases of fraud and corruption, involving losses of about £5.9 million. Primary care identified as high risk area for fraud. In hospitals, controls over income from private patients described as "exceptionally weak". More generally, some senior managers and non-executives are reluctant to acknowledge that there is a problem and many are inexperienced in dealing with it when they do encounter it.

5. Recommendations: Tighter checks on opticians, pharmacists and dispensing GPs. More involvement by all NHS Boards in dealing with fraud and corruption, with directors of finance submitting an annual report on the level of fraud and corruption and on the arrangements for preventing them. More emphasis on training staff on probity matters. Audit committees to ensure that internal audit has adequate resources.

Box 2 Patient Care Issues

Lying in wait: the use of medical beds in acute hospitals (1992)

1. Aim: to promote the more efficient use of acute hospital beds.

2. Methodology: Visits to 10 hospital acute units, information from three regional health authorities, a questionnaire survey of 100 acute units in England and Wales, national NHS statistics, published research reports. An advisory group of eight (clinicians, nurses, managers and analysts).

3. Target audience: managers and clinicians.

4. Findings: Wide variations in GP referrals, lengths of stay, discharge procedures. "If all districts could achieve lengths of stay and turnover intervals at least as low as the current best 25% (even after allowing for the effects of age), there would be the potential to provide the present level of activity in medicine with 58,000 beds rather than the 85,000 currently in use." Discharges often reflect the patterns of work of consultants with the result that patients may be "discharged too soon, too late or without adequate notice".

5. Recommendations: The report concludes with three pages of recommendations to managers and clinicians. These include - improving referral practices of GPs by use of protocols and better communication; coherent policies for placing and transferring patients, particularly the elderly; better management information and use of medical audit to review resource use and quality indicators; a review of consultant

discharge patterns and practices; a more flexible use of beds (including gender pooling).

Children First: A study of hospital services 1993

1. Aim: to monitor the implementation of government and professional guidelines designed to achieve an "integrated child health service".

2. Methodology: Detailed studies carried out in 10 district health authority sites and shorter visits were made to 10 hospitals in the UK and abroad, as well as to two regional health authorities. In addition, 28 other organisations were consulted. A survey of 48 families with children suffering from chronic conditions. An advisory group of 18 (predominantly paediatricians and nurses but also some pressure group representatives).

3. Target audience: managers, clinicians and the Department of Health.

4. Findings: The lack of written policies, management focus and poor communication means that "clinicians, managers and other staff do not give sufficient attention to the needs of children and their families". More doctors and nurses with paediatric expertise are needed: in 50% of wards, nurse staffing levels at night fail to achieve DoH standards. There is poor access to tertiary services. There are not enough separate facilities for children in A & E and out-patient departments. Outcomes of treatments (e.g. for glue ear) are not routinely monitored. High admission rates for asthma in some areas reflect a lack of guidelines and clarity about the role of GPs, parents and hospitals. There are wide variations in the average length of stay in paediatrics, even after taking account of differences in medical conditions: "If all hospitals could match

the length of stay achieved by hospitals in the lower quartile, occupied bed days in paediatrics would fall nationally by 10%".

5. Recommendations: Services should be better co-ordinated; more specially skilled staff should be available; facilities for both children and parents should be improved; the effectiveness of treatment should be monitored; clinicians should agree on guidelines for the management of glue ear (detailed recommendations on the procedures for making an initial diagnosis are included); more care and support should be provided in the home; the Department of Health should address the problem of inadequate national data and adopt a more rigorous approach to measuring the outcomes of health care.

United They Stand: Co-ordinating Care for Elderly Patients with hip fracture (1995)

1. Aim: To study the care received by elderly people with fractured hips.

2. Methodology: Nine hospitals visited and 450 patient records analysed. A group of hip fracture patients interviewed. Management of patients assessed against recommendations and guidelines produced by the Royal College of Physicians and other Royal Colleges. A 17 member Advisory Group, with strong professional representation (orthopaedic surgeons, nurses and therapists).

3. Target audience: Clinicians, managers, therapists, health authorities and trusts, social services agencies.

4. Findings: Hospitals failed to meet the Royal College of Physicians' recommendations in a number of respects: hip

fracture patients had to wait too long in A & E departments and many had to wait more than 24 hours to be operated on. Too many operations were carried out by unsupervised junior doctors. Discharge planning and policies were often inadequate. Patients did not feel sufficiently informed or involved in decisions about their care. Some models of good practice given.

5. Recommendations: Set clear standards for treating elderly people as the basis for audit; monitor and audit the number of operations performed by unsupervised junior doctors, the time taken before patients are operated on and the number of operations cancelled; establish standard assessment procedures for patients as the basis for planning and evaluating care; develop a formal multi-disciplinary team approach; ensure the availability of appropriate rehabilitation options.

Anaesthesia under examination: The efficiency and effectiveness of anaesthesia and pain relief services in England and Wales (1997)

1. Aim: to help spread information about good practice and to describe practical ways in which trusts can improve services and deal with problems of recruiting sufficient consultants (the topic was chosen because NHS trust chief executives voted it their top priority issue).

2. Methodology: Three national surveys of trusts to elicit information about a) availability/shortages of consultant anaesthetists b) anaesthetic cover in maternity services and c) pain relief services after surgery. A survey of patient experiences. Data collection in 39 acute trusts; managers and anaesthetists interviewed in seven trusts. An advisory group of 18 (President of the Royal College of Anaesthetists, various

clinicians and four members of the Audit Commission instead of the usual one).

3. Target audience: NHS Executive, chief executives and trust boards, clinical directors, directors of nursing, individual consultants and professional organisations.

4. Findings: Wide variations in staffing levels, grade mix, costs and productivity among anaesthetists and supporting staff suggesting scope for improving efficiency. Too many complex operations entrusted to junior doctors, particularly at night. Wide variations, too, in the availability of patient-controlled analgesia and in-patients reporting severe pain after surgery. Similarly with resources allocated to maternity services and to staffing chronic pain clinics.

5. Recommendations: Introduce explicit job plans for consultants, to be reviewed regularly; review grade mix of operating theatre staff; improve procedures for pre-operative patient preparation; monitor session cancellation rates, tighten rules for leave entitlements and control theatre staff sickness absence; devise guidelines for matching skills to patients; agree a policy for giving information to patients and offering them choice of anaesthetic, set targets for pain relief and introduce a programme of continuing education in pain management for trainee doctors and nurses; decide on the appropriate limits of clinical freedom (for example, what to do if guidelines agreed by the trust are not followed); sponsor research and pilot schemes to investigate the scope for using non-medically trained staff to administer anaesthesia.

First assessment: A review of district nursing services in England and Wales (1999)

1. Aim: To assist trusts and Primary Care Groups to assess existing services.

2. Methodology: National surveys of all trusts providing district nursing services and a sample (1500) of district nurses; a qualitative study of patients' and carers' experience of district nursing. Intensive fieldwork in seven NHS Trusts, involving caseload reviews of 21 district nursing teams, examination of more than 1600 activity diaries kept by district nurses and an analysis of data on more than 3400 referrals collected in a two-week prospective survey. An advisory group of 16 (seven nurses, GPs, a Help the Aged representative and three Audit Commissioners).

3. Target audience: Trust executives and nursing managers.

4. Findings: District nursing is an ill-defined, demand-led service: wide variations in referral rates reflect as much the practices of those referring (GPs and others) as the needs of the population. Similarly, different teams carry very different caseloads but these are rarely systematically reviewed. The quality of assessments varies widely, too, as between different trusts suggesting that there is scope for improving the quality of care also. In a working week of 37.5 hours, qualified district nurses spend 14 hours in contact with patients and 5.5. hours on patient management - with large variations, as always - so raising questions about whether they are making best use of their expensive time. Many examples of "good practice" given.

5. Recommendations: Managers must define objectives of service, improve referral process, review mix and use of skills, regularly evaluate case load and performance and ensure that

expensive clinical nurse specialist time is not used inappropriately. Peer review should be used to monitor the quality of assessment and audit outcomes; methods and frequency of collecting information about patient experiences need to be improved; efficiency gains could be achieved by making more use of clinics.

Box 3 - Household matters

Goods for Your Health: Improving Supplies Management in NHS Trusts (1996)

1. Aim: to improve efficiency of supplies procurement.

2. Methodology: The study was contracted out to a firm of management consultants. Fifteen trusts were studied by the consultants and shorter visits were made to a large range of other trusts and organisations, including suppliers, British Airways and the Confederation of British Industry. An advisory group of 16 (NHS executives and finance directors, as well as managers from the London Underground and Johnson & Johnson Medical).

3. Target audience: trust boards, senior management and clinicians.

4. Findings: Significant variations (as always) between trusts both in total supplies expenditure per patient and in the costs of procurement: some hospitals spend 50% more than others to treat a similar mix of patients. In about 25% of cases, the costs of ordering the item exceed its price. Trusts pay very different prices for identical goods; many trusts do not use competition sufficiently, neither do they aggregate orders. Equipment, once ordered, is often under-used. Better supplies management could release at least £150 million over three years.

5. Recommendations: Trust boards to take lead in planning supplies management, ensuring adequate information systems and training. In co-operation with clinicians, standardise consumables and equipment as far as possible. Eliminate small

package purchasing. Use competition wherever possible but also establish longer term suppliers wherever appropriate. Improve stock management, examine the causes of significant and unexplained variations in usage within the trust, increase equipment utilisation through effective pooling.

Getting Sorted: The safe and economic management of hospital waste (1997)

1. Aim: To assist hospitals in minimising costs while maintaining safe standards of waste disposal.

2. Methodology: Visits to 13 sites, supplemented by data collection from a further 16. An advisory group of 15 (NHS managers, representatives of the Health and Safety Executive and Environment Agency).

3. Target audience: hospital managers.

4. Findings: Large variations both in the quantity of waste produced per bed and in the cost of disposing of it. Staff frequently have little or no idea about the cost differences between the disposal of household and clinical waste, and often fail to segregate them. Arrangements for handling and storing waste are often unsatisfactory. Potential savings offered by better procedures are high: an estimated £250,000 a year for one teaching hospital visited.

5. Recommendations: These flow from the findings and include a long list of detailed recommendations about how to segregate and handle waste. In addition, the report recommends that hospitals should contract out waste disposal rather than investing in new incinerators. Good waste management requires the chief executive and the board to take the lead in devising effective and efficient procedures.

* *

Implicit in the Audit Commission's national VFM studies, as the examples suggest, is a set of assumptions about how decisions on the use and deployment of resources in the NHS should be taken. Irrespective of the particular topic under consideration, practice is in effect measured against a "rational actor" model of decision making. The chief requirements of the model are data about the distribution of resources, routine monitoring of how those resources are being used and information about outcomes as the necessary (though not sufficient) condition for taking rational decisions. Failing this, then there is a prima facie case for considering that resources are not being managed either efficiently or effectively. Hence the emphasis - running through all the Commission's national studies (Box 1) on improving information systems and devising performance targets and indicators. Hence, too, the depressing cumulative picture of an information-poor health service which frequently does not know what its staff are doing, whether the appropriate mix of skills is being used or how well the use of resources matches the needs of patients, let alone the relationship between inputs and outcomes.

Another defining characteristic of the Commission's studies is the use of data, whether drawn from national statistics or its own investigations, comparing the performance of different units. The point is further elaborated in the next section on methodology. Here it is sufficient to note that a guiding assumption is that variations in themselves demonstrate that there is scope for those at the bottom of any distribution to improve their performance by moving up to, or at least nearer, the level achieved by the "best", whether in terms of unit costs or lengths of stay or staffing levels. Thus in the case of children's services (Box 2), the report points out that occupied bed days in paediatrics could fall by 10% if all hospitals achieved the length of stay achieved by the top quarter. Similarly, the report on the use of medical beds in acute hospitals suggests that bed numbers could be cut radically if all providers matched the record of the "current best 25%". Overall, and with great consistency, the Commission's reports offer striking documentation and confirmation - if confirmation be needed - that variations in every aspect of performance are the norm in the NHS.

A third theme is an emphasis on the patient's perspective: on quality as perceived by the consumer. For this, the Audit Commission's studies have relied mainly on qualitative studies of small numbers of patients and consultation with patient advocacy groups. The latter are also frequently represented on advisory groups. More ambitiously, to take an example from one of the studies not included in our selective summaries, the Audit Commission commissioned a national survey of 3,570 recent mothers as part of its study of maternity services, designed to elicit the women's views about their experience. (10)

A fourth theme is the importance of strategic leadership, clearly defined objectives and lines of accountability. Again and again, the absence of these requirements is noted; conversely, the need for trust boards to take direct responsibility is stressed. So, for example, the first recommendation of the report on improving supplies management (Box 3) is that trust boards should "take ownership of supplies management, providing a framework and overall direction, linked to the trust's overall strategic objective". Here we are tapping another dimension of the "rational actor" model: i.e. the presumption that efficiency and effectiveness are dependent on the nature of the decision-making system in place.

There are other themes which feature frequently in the Audit Commission's report but which tend to be more contingent on the topic being studied. One of these is the importance of staff training, education and communication. So, for example, the need to analyse sickness absence patterns among staff as a first step to trying to reduce them is stressed. Another is the importance of co-ordination both within NHS trusts and between them and social services. The study of services for elderly patients with fractured hips (Box 2) illustrates the latter point.

Finally, our sample of reports underlines that the Commission's main concern is with the better use of public resources, not on reducing spending. There are indeed some reports which hold out the prospect of actual savings if the Audit Commission's recommendations are carried out. These fall into what we have labelled as the "household" category: supplies management (see Box 3) is a case in point. And they are very much the exception. In contrast, other studies - like the one on children's services - makes out the case for the investment of extra resources. Most reports come in an intermediate category, pointing out how existing resources could be used more efficiently and effectively if more authorities and trusts adopted "best practice" patterns: one of the main changes in the content and style of the reports has been the increasing prominence given, in the second half of the 1990s particularly, to identifying and citing named exemplars of "best practice" - i.e. providing templates of how to organise services. In this respect, the Commission's reports have moved from an analytic to a semi-prescriptive mode - the prescription being implicit in the selection of examples of good practice.

In all this, the Commission's hallmark is, as already indicated, a focus on the organisation and management of services. Again, we are back to the "rational actor" model: the question being put is what the necessary conditions are if sensible decisions are to be taken about the use of resources. Hence not only the emphasis on information but also the stress on the importance of clearly defined responsibilities, lines of accountability and so on. But many of the reports go beyond this kind of analysis. They also address substantive issues of service delivery: they make recommendations about skill-mix, the responsibilities of junior doctors, the role of nurses in anaesthesia and, perhaps an extreme example, how glue ear should be diagnosed. In short, it often appears to be questioning not just the organisational management of the NHS's resources but professional practice. This raises some more general questions about the role of the Commission How does it achieve credibility and legitimacy for its findings and recommendations? How does it, further, devise the criteria against which performance is assessed? Section 1.4 addresses these questions. But before that we look at the ways in which auditors examine themselves and test the quality and reliability of their audits.

1.3 Quality control of auditors and audit

In the case of private sector firms, quality control starts with the process of selection. There is an annual market testing of suppliers who respond to requests for bids to tender for audit services. Successful bids, based on price and quality record, are recommended through a panel to the governing board of the Commission. Once auditors have been appointed then the statutory duties are upon the auditor not the Commission. But the Commission remains responsible for ensuring the quality of the services being delivered, not least those offered by its own arm's length agency - District Audit.

Accordingly, the Commission has developed an elaborate Quality Control Review programme for auditors designed to ensure compliance with its Code of Audit Practice: a code setting out the "best professional practice of standards, procedures and techniques". In its mid-1990s form (11), the programme had three main components. First, independent reviewers examined the files of a sample of auditors' offices, grading the work done as very good, good, adequate or poor. Second, a number of chief executives were interviewed, an exercise complemented by a larger scale postal survey. Third, panels of readers examined a selection of management letters and other reports. On the basis of these reviews, the Commission produced a league table so that audit firms could see how they performed in relation to each other

In 1998 the Commission carried out a review of its QCR regime. The review included:

1. a stakeholder questionnaire - eliciting views of audit from audited bodies

2. an analysis of an annual cycle of performance indicators of audit

3. a summary of the findings of all quality control review (QCR) processes for the individual firms and districts.

Following this the Commission decided that the QCR system, in its original form, "had reached the end of its life cycle in terms of its ability to deliver further improvements" (12). Not only had the difference between the best and the worst audit firms been reduced to seven marks out of 100 but audited bodies satisfaction ratings had moved from 60% in 1993/1994 to 69% in 1996/1997. Accordingly, the Commission adopted a lighter touch approach. The league tables were dropped; the annual QCR cycle was turned into a five year one. And more emphasis was placed on risk-based reviews and the evaluation of the internal quality assurance systems of audit firms. In effect, the review has now been skewed away from a policing of auditors towards seeking their compliance; a fashion noticeable in the work of other inspectorates.

The main features of the scrutiny process remain unchanged, however. Quality control reviews are always headed up by someone brought into the Commission on secondment, either from a district audit office or from a private firm. Usually three or four reviews are being carried out at the same time and each review visit lasts two days. The reviews end up with a written report which is agreed with the audit firm being reviewed and there is a discussion about organisational performance. Reviewers also read a sample of management letters to audited bodies first to assess the quality and second to get an idea of what end product audited bodies are dealing with. The question is whether the management letter fulfils the Commission's requirements for accuracy as well as diplomacy: the management letter must not pull its punches but neither must it be written in too harsh tones.

"It is a high status document that is addressed to the audited body. It is a negotiated document which is addressed to the members of local authorities and boards of trusts and health authorities. It comments on outputs and the plans and interim reports of boards and it takes into account the long term, the medium term as well as the snapshot view of the authority."

Audit Commission official

The process of reviewing the Commission's QCR programme is a continuous one. The Commission is once again canvassing the opinions of audited bodies via questionnaires sent out to ask them what they think about the auditors who work in their area. Like other regulators, the Commission is concerned only with the quality of the audit itself as a technical exercise but also with the quality of the experience for the audited body. For, as we shall see in section 1.5, the impact of audit depends largely on how quality is perceived by the audited.

1.4 Constructing an Audit Performance: the case of two VFM studies

Given that audit is rarely - if ever - a straightforward exercise of checking performance against off-the-shelf standards, how do auditors devise the methods and the criteria of evaluation? What are the craft skills and processes involved in constructing the notion of good performance and achieving credibility for the audit? To answer these questions, we examine two recent Audit Commission reviews: those dealing with diabetes and critical care services respectively. These two cases were chosen in the expectation that auditing complex services for a chronic condition would be a more difficult task than auditing an exclusively hospital based acute service. In the event that expectation was not wholly fulfilled. If anything, the notion of "good performance" proved more elusive in the latter case. But between them the two reviews illustrate the nature of the task.

In what follows we look at the linked processes of preparing the Audit Commission's national study, producing a training manual for district auditors and organising training sessions to help them to carry out the subsequent local studies. Our information and observation on both VFM reviews comes from attending meetings of expert advisory groups and audit training sessions and discussions with the Audit Commission's central team members as well as from published material.

Diabetes services VFM Audit

A complete VFM study and audit cycle is an intricate and closely interwoven creation, carried out usually within an 18 months to two year period. The study of diabetes services began in March 1998 with the usual Audit Commission 'backgrounding' or collection of detailed information about the service. While this was happening, preparatory work was beginning on the national study and a pilot audit was set up. The pilot was completed in March 1999 and was used to inform the methodology and substance of the main audit which started at the beginning of 2000 and was due to finish in the Summer of 2000. The national study - *Testing Times: a review of diabetes services in England and Wales* - was published in April 2000.

The diabetes study had a mixed parentage. It was partly concern expressed by the British Diabetic Association about the variations in service quality and style throughout the NHS which put the topic on the Commission's agenda. The BDA is an organisation of and for patients, with a record of research as well as advocacy, so that from the beginning there was a strong user focus to the study:

> "The BDA is a strong national interest group which expects to be as influential as the Royal Colleges in setting standards."
>
> *VFM Central Team Member*

The decision to select diabetes as a study area also reflected an interest at the Department of Health in the state of services at the primary /secondary care interface. But equally the impetus for a VFM study and audit came from practitioners and service managers themselves at trust and authority level. Diabetes services emerged as an area of special importance and in need of a thorough public airing and examination. It fitted the programme requirements, therefore, and was selected by the Commission for inclusion in the programme for 1998. The justification for a study of diabetes was summed up in the Commission's national report:

> "Diabetes is a serious disease which accounts for about 9% of hospital costs, although total costs are much larger. It affects at least 3% of the population, although many more are undiagnosed, and numbers are rising rapidly."
>
> *Testing Times*

As part of the 'backgrounding' carried out at the beginning of the exercise, and in order to build a set of benchmarks for quality assessment, the advisory group (for membership see Box 4) and others met several times to hear about and comment on study proceedings. The groups provided a sounding board for team members to test what they were seeing as 'outsiders' (researchers and auditors) against how things appeared to 'insiders' (practitioners and patients) out in the field. The VFM study and pilot audits were thus information gathering exercises adjusted along the way by the observations and interpretations of users and experts. The extent of user involvement was high throughout. Not only were users strongly represented on the advisory group, but they also participated in auditor training where they advised auditors on the interpretation of cross-trust differences in service provision and helped the trainers to authenticate mock encounters between professionals and patients. No doubt this exceptional degree of user involvement reflected the special characteristic of people with diabetes: the fact that they are an active, articulate group with a strong, long-term self-interest in improving the quality of services - very different, in short, from the conventional stereotype of the passive patient.

> **Box 4 Membership of the diabetes advisory group**
> Three diabetics; two Department of Health/Welsh Office representatives; President of the Royal College of General Practitioners and two other GPs;chair of the Royal College of Nursing Diabetes Forum and one other nurse; a Professor of Health Psychology; five consultants; Director of Care, British Diabetic Association; a diabetic services co-ordinator; Chairman of Council of Society of Podiatrists; a dietician.

The field work focused on hospitals, since the aim of the exercise was to produce tools for the local audit of acute trusts as well as a national study. The study teams visited nine hospitals, spending three to four days at each. At each hospital, data was collected about diabetes services, patient records were reviewed and staff interviewed. In addition, two postal surveys were carried out: one of people with diabetes, the other of general practices corresponding to each of the nine hospital sites. The team also made 30 short visits to academic research departments, professional bodies, patient groups and health authorities. Finally, a telephone survey was carried out of 26 health authorities to establish the profiles of all diabetes services in the area. Like the survey of GPs, this represented recognition of the fact that a study of diabetes could not be confined to acute services but would have to cover primary care as well.

Discussions at advisory meetings did not produce a consensus about how an ideal model of service provision should be organised in the sense of specific numbers and types of staff involved. Given the heterogeneity of the interests represented, this was only to be expected. So the production of such a definitive model, against which performance can then be assessed, awaits the publication of the government's national service framework for diabetes in 2001. How, then, was performance to be assessed in the absence of such a template? The answer lay in getting agreement, based on research evidence and examples of good practice, about what the essential goals and components of such a model should be. So, for example, the research evidence demonstrated that good education and support improved long-term outcomes and that regular checks of eyes, feet and other tests can ensure the early detection of complications so minimising their effects. As the national study report put it:

> "The good news is that there is sound evidence about what works. We know that good management can reduce the risk of serious complications and lengthen life. This means prompt diagnosis, regular checks to identify serious complications at an early stage, and treatment to control blood glucose and blood pressure levels. Support and education is crucial so that individuals can manage this complex disease effectively themselves."

From the evidence, buttressed by the views of users, flowed a series of questions or criteria. How far did services promote and sustain self-management? How easy or difficult was access to advice and treatment, particularly for ethnic minorities? Were hospitals supporting diabetes care in the community? Were there adequate programmes for retinal screening and for detecting foot problems? And once detected, were problems referred to hospitals quickly enough? If treated in hospital, were the special needs of patients with diabetes recognised?

The national study also drew on the Audit Commission's standard repertory of criteria for assessing any NHS service or programme. Did health authorities and trusts have the information systems required for monitoring and planning services? Was there adequate co-ordination between the different components of the service? Were there guidelines for GP referrals to hospital? Was there a well-developed programme of education for staff?

Predictably, the national study reported that - as always - there were wide variations on all these dimensions of performance between trusts, health authorities and GP practices. Most of the report's recommendations were, further, based on and illustrated by examples of existing good practice. To a large extent the notion of "good performance" was therefore constructed on the basis of existing best practice in the NHS. This, of course, begs the question of how best practice is defined. Here the Audit Commission - as already noted - could claim legitimacy in terms of research evidence, expert advice and user views, reinforced by an extensive consultation process once a draft report had been produced. And although most of the report dealt with the delivery of clinical services, it did so in terms of how these should be organised, monitored and co-ordinated without challenging the way in which clinicians practised their craft.

The questions shaping the national study report also provided the agenda for the local auditors. They also suggested some essential elements of good practice and these were set out in the very detailed audit guide which gave auditors step by step advice on how to conduct themselves during an audit as well as how to carry out the audit itself.

The audit training guide first set out to teach auditors about diabetes and familiarise them with the disease. A profile of the disease was given which included, for example, information on types of diabetes, the numbers of people suffering and the complications of the condition. An account was given of the range of services auditors would be likely to encounter. The guide also outlined a structure of the audit and what would be involved in carrying it out. For example, auditors would arrive at an overview of services in a health trust by using patients' case notes, carrying out patient surveys, looking at the structure of staffing for the service and at the interface between primary and secondary services. In the section on aims and approaches to audit, the guide justified the diabetes audit by referring to the status of the disease in the NHS - historically labelled one of the 'cinderella services - and the potential for reducing fragmentation of service delivery and improving co-ordination between different parts.

The guide advised auditors on the timing of the exercise and the importance of getting the right skill mix of auditors to carry out the job. Auditors were also advised on the 'etiquette' of audit. That is, making themselves familiar with the trust being scrutinised, setting up meetings with the right people - establishing a high level contact or sponsor is vital for a successful audit - and explaining themselves and their tasks very carefully and clearly to the auditees. There was a particular emphasis on presenting themselves as knowledgeable and in control without appearing arrogant and superior.

The scope and boundaries of an audit were also emphasised. Auditors were told what they can and cannot ask: what is legitimate audit business and what falls outside their remit, authority and expertise. This includes not only the limitations of auditors within audit generally but also boundaries very specific to the service under review. For example, a diabetes audit must find out about barriers to access to the service: language barriers for non English speaking patients, out of hours access barriers and those for people with physical disabilities.

Finally the audit guide summarised what was known about good practice in diabetes services so that auditors could offer this to trusts, especially those with less than good practice, for discussion and negotiation. Good practice definitions included, smooth and speedy referrals between hospital department and particularly between primary and secondary services, and minimal delays when complications of the disease arise.

But examples of good practice, as was stressed during the training sessions for local auditors, could not be used in an automatic or formulaic way: they should be used as tin-openers rather than dials (13) That is, areas of service activity can be highlighted by audit as requiring further exploration while at the same time accepting there is no way of directly measuring performance. Introducing the local auditors to the technicalities of diabetes care, a hospital consultant warned that a bad service can display some of the same elements as a good service and they should not fall into the trap of false images and narrow contexts. There are, in other words, many complexities to observe and assess, for example the ambiguous implications of specific staffing in health services. On the one hand, consultant led services can be an indicator of good practice since medical leadership denotes a focused interest in a trust. On the other hand, consultant led services are not always a good sign for a service:

"While it is a positive indicator for some services and specialities, a strong consultant presence does not always signal well. For example, where consultants are trying to build their specialism locally for personal reasons rather than the good of the service or the interests of patients."

"This does not mean, of course, that performance indicators cannot be devised for service assessment. It does mean, however, that auditors have to use them carefully and in conjunction with other information about the service and the specific circumstances in which the service is being delivered."

Consultant Trainer

In summary, then, in the case of the diabetes services, the audit exercise successfully identified criteria by which the performance of the NHS could be judged, without however translating these into an organisational model or measurable indicators of success. Much was left to the discretion of district auditors in applying the criteria to local circumstances. Issues of economy, efficiency and effectiveness in the delivery of services were not explicitly addressed; the presumption shaping the exercise appears to have been that these would be a by-product of delivering appropriate, high quality services. To test whether these characteristics of the exercise flow from its focus on a chronic service, or reflect the Audit Commission's overall style, we next turn to examine the VFM study of critical care services.

Critical Care VFM Audit

The critical care VFM study and audit began in late 1997, roughly at the same time as the diabetes study. There were some interesting differences between them, however. First, whereas the diabetes audit had been brought into the Commission programme as a free standing project, critical care had already been discussed as a natural adjunct to the anaesthesia and pain relief services study completed in 1997. In the event, they were separated and carried out sequentially. Because some of the background work had been done, the consultation exercise of the critical care study, therefore, was carried out in a shorter time period than the diabetes study. The central team held only two advisory meetings, one midway through January and the second in June 1998.

But if the advisory meetings were fewer in critical care than in the diabetes study, the fieldwork was on a larger scale. The VFM team researched the study thoroughly, employing a wide range of methods. These included detailed visits to six sites, a national survey of all trusts, a targeted sample of trusts, a survey of consultants with sessional commitments to intensive care units and a data set of self selected trusts provided by the Intensive Care National Audit and Research Centre(ICNARC). A draft specification was drawn up in October 1997 and a consultation draft produced in December 1997. A pilot audit guide was produced in April 1998, when the first pilot audit workshop was also held - in preparation for the district audit planned for 1999. The report of the national study was published in 1999: *Critical to success: The place of efficient and effective critical care services within the acute hospital.*

Critical care VFM was, thus, propelled into existence relatively more speedily than the diabetes study while consulting with a smaller but professionally more high powered advisory group. Out of 16 advisory team members, 11 were medically qualified, two were nurses and a further two were trust chief executives. There was also one solitary ex-intensive care unit patient. By definition, ICU survivors do not (in contrast to diabetes sufferers) form a homogenous, active group of users with a long-term interest in improving the service.

The second major difference between the two exercises was that the impetus for a study of critical care services had come largely from within NHS management. Trust chief executives had expressed disquiet about the resourcing of critical care and its effects on surgical services generally. In contrast to the study of diabetes services - largely shaped by a concern with patient interests - the critical care study was thus primarily driven by a search for greater management control over the effective and efficient use of resources. The aims of the exercise, as set out in the study specifications, were to improve:

1. strategic planning and operational management of critical care

2. the appropriate use of critical care beds

3. the efficiency with which staff are deployed

4. the quality of patients' and relatives' experiences.

In carrying out the study, the central VFM team faced the fundamental problem of defining critical care, not only for audit purposes but also to produce a checklist of criteria against which performance could be assessed. As one member of the VFM team put it:

"What is critical care? There are no fixed national standards as we discovered in the fieldwork. All trusts and critical care units have their own definitions. What we do know is that critical care is about high levels of staff, high technology equipment, high mortality and high stress. But precise levels of staff vary, equipment varies, admissions, discharges and definitions of appropriate patients and appropriate treatments vary from unit to unit."

"Some critical care units are managed by a director but most are free resources for the whole trust and, as a result, have no management in place. Doctors make individual decisions about who is admitted and discharged and which treatments are given. Some units are so unstructured that treatments change from one day or week to the next as different doctors go on and off duty."

"Bed numbers and nursing staff ratios also vary historically. The meaning of 'sufficient nurse numbers' varies around the country according to the way the unit calculates their nurse/patient ratios. There is no national standard for this so the range of variations is great, from 1 to 1 up to 8 to 1. The site visits even found one trust which had 9 nurses to one patient as a working ratio in its critical care unit."

Given variations in the number and types of ICU units, in the case-mix of patients treated, in levels of pattern of staffing and in outcomes - given, in short, the sheer heterogeneity of the service - how could audit assess performance? In contrast to diabetes, there could be little appeal to evidence. The national report pointed out that "there is a lack of scientific information about which interventions are effective" and recommended that "more effort should be put into researching why patients live or die". The answer (very much in line with general Audit Commission practice) was to re-define the problem as a solution. Variations would provide the mirror in which trust managers could examine their own performance: managers would be given data showing how their costs compared to similar units and analysing how much variations in cost are due to differences in nurse staffing standards, grade mix, shift systems and proportions of nurses involved in direct patient care as well as medical staffing levels. Once again, data was the tin-opener.

But the findings of the various visits and surveys also identified specific aspects of performance that required attention from auditors and managers once the tin had been opened. The use of nurses - the largest single element in the cost of providing critical care - prompted a series of questions. Why, for example. was a high proportion of nursing time devoted to re-assuring the relatives, rather than minding the patients or watching high technology equipment? And what was the rationale for the different mixes and levels of staffing? Was there scope for using staff more flexibly? And there were other issues. What were the criteria for allocating patients to critical care beds as distinct from the cheaper high or even low dependency beds? The audit visits had found it difficult to distinguish between the patients in the different types of beds. Were there adequate guidelines and processes for taking ethically difficult decisions about refusing admission to critical care for patients unlikely to benefit and for withdrawing treatment? And were relatives given adequate explanations for such decisions?

The focus in all this, the Audit Commission stressed, was to be on economy, efficiency and effectiveness in the way critical care units operated, not on clinical management or clinical outcomes. But there was a contradiction in this. As the national study report put it:

> "Critical care may become the backstop for a poorly performing hospital. Poor general care can result in patients needing critical care. This inflates the number of critical care beds required. Poor care may happen in A & E, the admissions unit, the operating theatre or on the wards. It can happen due to organisational failures, communication breakdowns, failure to seek consultant or specialist advice, failure to spot or act on danger signs, and failures in supervision and on-call response."

The implication was clear. Any audit of critical care would have to dig deep into the organisational and clinical structure of a trust: how, for example, could the demand for critical care beds be discussed without reference to the clinical practices which sent patients to them? The point was reinforced in the audit guide which, as always, drew on the rational actor model of decision making. Here local auditors were advised that:

> "One of the conclusions that you are likely to reach is that your trust needs to plan its critical care services corporately and integrate its plans better with those of all aspects of the organisation and delivery of services for acutely ill patients. The emphasis is on planning to meet the needs of patients rather than on the needs of the people who provide the services. The approach cuts across existing departmental boundaries and will require changes in culture as well as to structures and processes."

The guide not only followed the detailed and comprehensive format common to other Commission audit manuals, it also contained very specific instructions on the dangers of breaching the boundaries of a critical care audit. For example, the focus of the advice to auditors was on standing back from overt criticism of trusts, and rather helping them to understand the implications of their activities for good and bad practice. The guide strongly recommended a 'hands-off' approach for auditors in discussions with trust management of, particularly, staffing levels and service configuration.

Potentially, then, the local audit of critical care promised to be an extremely challenging, subversive and hence explosive exercise. From this flowed some of the anxieties expressed by auditors in the training sessions. There were two main concerns. First and foremost, auditors were worried about their own credibility with trusts, critical care departments and, in particular, with professional staff. They were uncertain as to the parameters of the audit vis-à-vis professional decisions about services. Losing face at the beginning of the audit process was anticipated by auditors when asking skilled professionals what they were doing and why.

The second biggest concern of auditors was the reliability of the data they were expected to interpret and discuss, or challenge NHS staff with. Again, a loss of credibility was anticipated as a result of using inappropriate data for audit purposes. The questions at the training session reflected these concerns:

> "Supposing the data were not accurate? Some staff and trusts are not interested in comparative data and others deny the reliability of data produced by audit. Are the performance indicators robust enough to present to trusts and critical care units?"

Auditors were particularly unclear as to the status of an efficiency and effectiveness audit that placed limits on critically examining staffing levels and costs:

> "What are the boundaries of audit? What can I look at and comment on if critical questions to do with staffing levels are not our concern?"

The replies of the central team to the concerns of auditors about this particular boundary in the critical care audit were that auditors could only point out that some trusts had different staffing levels to others, and could only suggest to trust managers and clinicians that they explore these carefully and reflect on the implications for services to patients. The auditor with the grave doubts about his role was concerned that it was not part of his job to "question" staffing levels rather than merely ask questions. The central team placed great emphasis on auditors helping managers and professionals to see connections between staffing levels and good or bad practice for themselves.

Audit Commission central team experience of site visits and the pilot audit covered both general concerns and those specific to a critical care audit. High on the training agenda was an acknowledgement that audit is an uncertain task, made even more stressful when carried out in strong professional territory such as critical care services. As a member of the VFM central team put it:

"Auditors will come up against lobbies and staff interest groups and must understand clearly that there are a number of agenda operating within a trust and within a critical care unit itself. Auditors must be aware of the key issues being discussed by staff at present in the NHS. ie shortage of beds, particularly critical care beds, and nursing staff shortages. The evidence so far from the VFM study is that staffing and bed situations vary around the country and that the 'shortage' is at present a talking point which has yet to be proved a reality. But the VFM audit in the NHS is tricky and the Audit Commission would not want to understate the difficulties of this study for auditors."

Overall, the auditors at the training sessions on critical care were not fed many reassurances about their audit role by the VFM central team. Its members had found during their initial site visits that trust managers wanted some comparative information on critical care units to help them gain management control over their own unit. Some managers did not even know what the structure of their own unit looked like or what it did exactly. Managers were particularly concerned to know about variations between types and grades of staff on a comparative basis. Since this audit was initiated largely by and for managers of trusts, the VFM central team told auditors at the training sessions that they would be facing an efficiency and effectiveness audit of a service where, by and large, no-one is in managerial control and there are no guidelines on staffing or patient admission and discharge. Further, the problem of futile surgery and terminal care use of beds goes largely without discussion, as do ethical and managerial issues.

The Audit Commission central team finished the training by telling auditors what they could, couldn't or should do at a critical care audit. Starting with a sensible suggestion for anyone fetching up in a strange and uncertain situation, auditors were urged first to find themselves a high level sponsor on immediate arrival at a trust and to use the sponsor to check the accuracy of the data base for audit. They were then advised, in the words of one of the central team, on their conduct and demeanour during an audit:

> "Auditors must present themselves in a good light, as flexible and diplomatic thinkers and workers. They must be clear about the scope of the audit and their duties and they must find the right people to talk to. They must be aware that critical care staff see themselves as highly skilled. They must also be aware that the situation is complex, tricky and stressful, and they must be aware of different agendas and lobbies."

> "Make sure you produce an accurate comparative data report. Go through everything with your sponsor. Remember that standards and staffing levels are professional views of what is appropriate, not national standards or even trust standards, but equally not the business of the audit."

The national study report, *Critical to Success*, echoed the trickiness and apparent contradictions in the audit role. It reflected the fact that the construction of this audit was conjured out of the difficult to define concept of critical care services. And more importantly, that the audit had, quite properly, produced questions rather than answers to critical care issues:

"The report is not a blueprint for the reconfiguration of the country's network of services. It does not consider the number of beds needed nationally, the workings of the National Intensive Care Bed Register, whether current patterns of transfer between hospitals are appropriate, or how to transfer patients safely. Instead, the Audit Commission's recommendations are aimed at helping individual trusts to improve their services."

Comparing the two audits

Given the two quite different origins of the two studies, we could hypothesise that critical care with its high density (and high status) medical expertise would be politically more difficult to construct and more tricky for auditors to carry out than the more diffuse (and lower status) diabetes services. That is, critical care auditors would be more likely to be confronting providers who perceived audit as threatening. On the other hand, because the critical care audit was more clearly about the efficient and effective use of resources, it could equally mean that auditors were working in their professional element to a greater extent than they were in diabetes services.

In the outcome, both audits were constructed out of slippery concepts of service provision, uncertain boundaries, and with the challenge of arriving at definitions of good practice. In this respect, there was a level of convergence in issues and dilemmas for auditors to cope with in the diabetes and critical care studies. But whereas the former did identify some good practices linked to good service outcomes, the latter remained more uncertain as to the definition of critical care and service outcomes and turned its audit task into raising questions for providers and managers, at all levels in the NHS, to find answers. There were other differences as well, notably in the degree to which the user perspective could be incorporated into the exercise and the degree to which economy, efficiency and effectiveness were stressed. Most significantly, however, both exercises underline one general conclusion about the nature of audit in the NHS. This is that the auditor's craft depends on skill in negotiating the often elusive and ambiguous meaning of "performance" and diplomacy in treading the delicate path between the traditional audit preoccupation with the three Es and professional practice.

1.5 Impact of audit

Is the NHS more efficient or effective in the way it uses resources as a result of the Audit Commission's VFM activities? What difference have the many national studies and the follow-up inquiries of local auditors made to the way in which the NHS operates? Does the Commission itself deliver value for money? In a sense, these are the only questions about the Commission that matter. Unfortunately, they are also questions that are impossible to answer with precision or certainty. The reason is simple. The NHS is in a constant process of change. Those working in it are under a variety of pressures - ministerial, budgetary, bureaucratic and professional - to improve the way in which they work. Attempting to attribute credit for improvements in performance (however defined or measured) to any single actor in the crowded theatre of the NHS is therefore a doomed enterprise. If the Audit Commission has a catalytic role in prompting change - as it certainly does - its own effectiveness depends on the complex chemistry, local and national, of particular topics. If the Audit Commission has a role in putting issues on the action agenda of ministers and managers - as it certainly does - its effectiveness again depends on the receptivity and sensitivity of others to particular issues. In neither case is it possible to isolate and thus to quantify, even in the broadest terms, the Commission's individual contribution.

In what follows, we do not attempt, therefore, to assess the "impact" of the Commission in terms of the difference that it has made to the way in which the NHS organises and uses resources. For the reasons given above, that would be an impossible task. Instead, we report on the Commission's own attempts to measure its effectiveness and on our fieldwork designed to elicit how the Commission's work was perceived in the NHS. In both cases, as we shall see, effectiveness tends to be assessed in terms of process rather than outcome: i.e. the focus is on the extent to which audit succeeds in engaging the audited in a process of change rather than on identifiable results in organisational or financial terms.

The Audit Commission's own assessment.

The Audit Commission has carried out two studies of the impact of its VFM activities on the NHS. The first was carried out by the Commission's Health Studies Branch (recently abolished) in 1997 (14). The review took the form of detailed interviews with trust personnel involved with audits undertaken over the previous three years in 12 trusts. In each of these trusts two audits had been undertaken - of medical staffing and radiology - by the same audit team but one had been deemed successful and the other unsuccessful.

The purpose of this review was to inform the HS branch strategy for developing VFM audit and to improve the quality of current audit materials: to understand better what makes for a local VFM study audit that delivers change; and conversely what obstacles prevent change. The review looked at auditor credibility, developing and agreeing audit recommendations and securing action by trusts as essential parts of an effective audit process.

Auditor credibility was a high priority on trusts' requirements for a VFM audit. Some chief executives interviewed were concerned about the lack of NHS experience of VFM auditors visiting their trusts. It was clear that one poor piece of audit work could sour relations between audit and audited more or less permanently. Failure by the auditors to get the audit clearly understood plus uncertainty about the audit timetable was identified by some trusts as a serious problem.

Where audits were thought to have been successful, significant time was spent by auditors in discussing findings and preparing reports. It is the process rather than the quality of the final report which affects the trusts' perceptions that an audit was successful or a failure. Trusts also had strong reservations about the way auditors presented recommendations for action. Comments were made that recommendations were too vague, too many and added up to an indigestible change agenda. Comparative data was not acceptable to many trusts unless it came from primary sources, i.e. not from centrally gathered returns.

However, the quality of the audit itself was only one factor in determining the outcome (as measured by the implementation of the auditors' recommendations) of the process. The other was the characteristics of the trust being audited. If the chief executive was sceptical about the whole notion of VFM audit (as was the case in three out of the twelve trusts), then there was little point in proceeding with it. Similarly, audit was unlikely to be successful unless it fitted into the trust's own change agenda. Finally, staff turnover in trusts and a constantly changing (and overloaded) national agenda compounded the difficulties.

Overall, the review concluded that "implementation of auditor's recommendations was generally disappointing". In the case of radiology about a quarter of the recommendations had been fully implemented: in the case of medical staffing, the proportion fell to one tenth. Given that such recommendations are usually negotiated and agreed with trust management, this is indeed a disappointing result. And it becomes more so given that even these figures may be over-optimistic. One trust manager was quoted as remarking "how easy it was to get the auditor to agree that recommendations had been implemented when in fact no action had been taken". And the review noted that "a major shortcoming in the audit process" was "the absence of any thorough and detailed review of previous recommendations" and the failure of subsequent management letters to alert non-executive directors to lack of progress.

A different methodology, using national performance indicators, was adopted in a later study by the Commission published in 1999 (15). This looked at the changes in practice subsequent on five of the Commission's NHS VFM studies: day surgery, A & E services, radiology, mental health and the use of water in hospitals. Only in two cases, day surgery and water use, was progress in implementing the recommendations classified as "good" without qualifications; in two others, radiology and A & E services, progress was described as either "poor" or "mixed" and two had produced little or no change. The study concluded, however, that many factors underlie changes in trust activities after a VFM audit. These include:

• The extent to which a study is in harmony with government and professional thinking

• The quality of local auditors' work

• The capacity of local bodies to implement change

These qualifications underline - as the study itself fully recognises - the problems of trying to use national performance indicators (or statistical data of any kind) as a dial for measuring the Audit Commission's own performance as a change agent. Too many other factors, as argued in the introduction to this section, are involved. The only variables under the Commission's control are the quality of local auditors' work and the menu of studies offered to trusts. Not surprisingly, therefore, the study concluded by suggesting that the Commission's priority should be to identify more precisely why there are differences in the impact of its studies and to build the results into its study and inspection processes.

Indeed this is a direction in which the Commission is already going, with the emphasis on ensuring the credibility (and therefore the acceptability) of its VFM studies within the field. As a by-product of the quality assurance process (see section 1.3 above) the recently set up performance development unit is identifying the basis for a "good" inspection, drawing on the evidence of the Quality Control Review and complaints. Charts have been prepared from survey data of audited bodies which show the things that can go wrong with an audit. The first diagram used by the unit is of a "vicious cycle" of audit and the second shows a "virtuous cycle". In the words of one of the unit's staff:

> "It is when the auditor turns up at a trust and meets the top people (chief executive, finance director and clinical director) that a 'bell rings' and everything goes either up or down from there on. The initial chemistry between the auditor and the audited body sets the tone and the path and the pace for the entire audit. The word goes around and down the line that 'an idiot/idiots are in the building' and the audit is given no co-operation. As a result, the audit schedules get later, the programme slips and the whole thing gets more expensive as the days to complete increase. The reports are then late, as is the management letter, and the trust ends up with a bad and expensive audit experience."

The quotation reinforces the theme of this section: that not only is the impact of the Audit Commission's VFM work difficult to identify and isolate but it is also highly contingent. The diplomatic skill and professional know-how of local auditors is a necessary but far from sufficient condition for opening the doors to change - but will not, in themselves, ensure that managers and clinicians actually walk through that door.

The view from the audited

In this section we report on how audit was perceived by the audited. We define "impact" in terms of the impression made on those working in the NHS. Five hospital trusts, four health authorities and two regional authorities were studied and a range of staff, including chief executives and directors of finance were canvassed about their audit experiences and those of their organisation. Discussions were also held with the Confederation of Health Authorities and Trusts on their interpretations of how their members viewed VFM audit in the NHS.

Given some indications of questions about local audit if not complaints from members, the Confederation had not much actual evidence of hostility towards the Audit Commission at grass root level. One of the reasons for this lack of evidence is that Confederation surveys of members usually have a very low response rate and the survey of audit reactions was exceptionally low. The assumption is that trusts and health authorities do not respond to surveys unless they are interested. The general impression at headquarters is that although national VFM studies are highly regarded, local district auditors are seen as more varied. Inter-team variability of audit is an NHS issue.

Another Confederation general impression is that it is medical consultants who grumble most about VFM audit. A case was cited of the VFM Maternity Services Inquiry which produced very different reactions in two trusts. One London trust had no time for it and declared it to be rubbish while a neighbouring trust said the report was excellent. The Confederation learned that the report went against the local practices at the first trust which were reflected by the dominant position of a particular consultant. The department said it was a bad audit although its recommendations followed national guidelines for good practice.

In summary, the Confederation's view is that trusts vary in their response to audit but that VFM is probably the least popular audit. And, by and large, trusts complain vaguely about being over-audited, although audit is now part of the NHS landscape. On the ownership of audit, the Confederation noted that its history is complex and that the audited body is the client and yet not. Trusts are monitored externally and without choice while at the same time being clients who are consulted and accommodated. Not surprisingly, the Confederation does not think it plays a big enough part in the audit of its members. In particular, as one official pointed out, it would like to be allowed into the audit process early enough to be a key player:

> "We should be part of the scoping process. We share in the draft reports on national studies and we go to some advisory meetings at the Audit Commission. We get a prior to publication report when it is too late to change things. We would want to change a report if it missed the point. For example, we would have changed the emphasis in the report on clinical governance. The Audit Commission missed the crunch in their critical care study because the Confederation was excluded from the early stages. As a result the report is not punchy enough."

The views of audit and VFM audit from the audited bodies showed - predictably - considerable variations in the degrees of perceived usefulness of audit and the amount and types of aggravation reported. There was, however, a consensus among general managers that the Audit Commission itself had made progress in recent times on focusing VFM audit more clearly on issues of real interest to trusts and local providers of health services:

"The work of the Audit Commission has been very helpful and contributed a lot to the running of the NHS. The central issues that it has identified have been just that - very central to the problems of the NHS. Some of the reports - Accident & Emergency, Outpatients etc. - have been completely appropriate as topics and so readable. But the readability factor applies to all their publications."

Chief Executive, Health Authority

Managers were also pleased that they could now negotiate with the Commission on which VFM studies were relevant in their local areas. Full VFM audits can be dispensed with in favour of preliminary audits and topics can be negotiated:

"We have a choice of audit topics up to a point. We can steer auditors into specific areas if the favoured topic does not suit."

Chief Executive, Hospital Trust

The Commission was said to have sensible audit dialogue with trusts and health authorities where there was a sufficient level of trust. Certainly, the VFM pre-audit national studies were thought to be technically good and useful levers for change - and confrontation - for managers. But if VFM audits gave managers levers for tackling difficult problems, they could also introduce extra pressures for changes within existing resource restraints and competing priorities:

> "The choice of topics for VFM studies and audits, coming as they do from the Audit Commission, may not coincide with existing local and national priorities."
>
> *Regional Director*

One general manager of a hospital trust described using a VFM audit as a lever to override a clinical practices audit system in place which was counter-productive for general management:

> "The results of a VFM audit enabled management to tackle a clinical audit system which was frankly a farce - so we got rid of it. The getting rid would not have been possible earlier because, however farcical, the doctors would not agree to get rid. Before the VFM audit, the good doctors were auditing their own clinical practices using clear guidelines - and doing it well. But unfortunately, the bad doctors were doing nothing."
>
> *Chief Executive, Hospital Trust*

Whereas this was a single case of very positive reaction to audit encountered in the study, most of the senior managers asked about VFM audit were concerned more about the variability of district auditors carrying out VFM studies - public and private - and how unsatisfactory auditors made for a bad audit:

> "The most difficult thing about district audit is the variable quality of individual auditors. But we - that is any of the directors of the trust - can request an auditor specifically even within a district audit."
>
> *Chief Executive, Hospital Trust*

> "Our current auditors are hopeless....no help at all. They don't understand the structural problems which cause financial problems in the NHS. They look at whether the computer system is working and whether the financial

control system is sound but they don't understand change management."

Chief Executive, Health Authority

But even those senior managers who talked of variable quality of VFM audit noted that there has been some improvement over time as both the Commission and local auditors have become more skilled. A chief executive who remembered the early days of VFM audit went further saying that the improvements were not just on the part of the auditors but also in the audited bodies responses to audit:

"In the past the quality of individuals undertaking VFM at district level has been variable - especially when VFM first started. But the quality has improved and things have been getting better over the last 3-4 years. Both Audit Commission and district audit - and trusts for that matter - have learned to be flexible and now handle VFM studies quite professionally."

Chief Executive, Hospital Trust

More hope for better audit was suggested by a health authority chief executive who suggested that a level of trust between auditors and auditees was essential for a good or successful audit. And where there is little trust it may be that some audited bodies have not earned it:

"What clients want from auditors is increasing responsiveness and this is what has been happening recently with the Audit Commission. However, the Commission relaxes its rigidity only where they have confidence in the audited bodies - so inevitably district audit is more relaxed with some health authorities and trusts than others."

Chief Executive, Health Authority

A high level of trust was cited by two chief executives, one of a health authority and one of a hospital trust, as the result of a particular culture and management style. Trusting one another within the authority - doctors and managers included - had given an air of confidence to their financial management as well as service provision. As a direct result, auditors have always trusted and been trusted in return. Confidence and trust go hand in hand in the NHS and this reflects on the quality of an external audit:

> "Thinking about audit as a complete system, we have a comfortable working relationship internally in the trust which means that general management, financial management, medical directors and audit get on together and discuss all aspects of money and audit. We have a brilliant audit committee which is helpful. When I say we all get on, I don't mean we cover things up or ignore problems. The good working relationship means we can all be honest and constructive. We have been rated by the Audit Commission and the district audit as an organisation that is sound financially and strategically: we are working well together as an organisation and heading in the right direction according to our resources."
>
> *Chief Executive, Hospital Trust*

On a similar if slightly different note, a chief executive of a health authority was puzzled about the concept of problems with external audit. It had never occurred to this chief executive to start off an audit in an indifferent or hostile manner. In the last ten years, he had never been sent an unintelligent external auditor: inexperienced but not unintelligent. He summed up by saying that audit is all about trust like most other activities in organisations:

> "I cannot recall any major battles with auditors in all my years in the NHS. Not even at senior management level. I

have been in discussions with outside auditors to decide what VFM study we are going to do but it is always a negotiation rather than an argument. If they want to do the 'flavour of the month' VFM audit and it is not appropriate to us, then I will tell them what we have in mind and come to some arrangement and agreement. Either we agree on another topic or we agree to a smaller study at a later date. As long as I justify my preferences then the audit is happy to go along with things. All we have to do is make a case for what we need or want at the time."

Chief Executive, Health Authority

An additional slant was given to the concept of auditor variations by a director of finance at a hospital trust:

"There are no real audit problems which can be generalised around the country. Apart from the shift to VFM away from probity - which is now tipping back anyway. There are too many variations in the quality of audit, quality of auditors and the relationship between these and the audited bodies to point to any one outstanding area of dissatisfaction. There are no geographical pockets of problems as far as I know."

Director of Corporate Services, Hospital Trust

Senior managers, both chief executives and directors of finance had a few suggestions for the Audit Commission to take on board in what was generally thought to be an improved system of VFM studies and audit. These were mainly add-ons rather than radical changes. For example, a Regional Director suggested that the Commission should add more short and snappy studies - quick snapshot jobs - to its VFM programme in areas where speed of findings is crucial for NHS policy.

The regional directors especially were thinking of ways to improve the system of regional management in the NHS, some via the Audit Commission. Thus one director suggested that the Audit Commission could help even if the management job of regions largely rested on informal trust:

> "My region is fortunate in having made voluntary agreements with trusts and health authorities that they will share their audit reports with one another and with the region. But if comparisons could be made between audits based on local needs this would improve the region's capacity for performance management - even for those regions which already have access to their health authorities' and trusts' audit reports. The Audit Commission should produce a regional digest of audit findings so that (a) trusts and health authorities could be compared within a region and (b) provide an aggregate of all trust and health authority performances so that a review can be done of a regional performance. Eventually this will have to be done to allow regions to manage performance. There are services which can only be monitored on a regional basis; for example, intensive care services which are not justified on trust by trust basis. Not every hospital can be self sufficient in all service provision in spite of government emphasis on eliminating 'post code rationing' in the NHS. My region will be monitoring the regional programme for intensive care services and requires, therefore, a regional network system of audit to do this."

Regional Director

A second regional director also expressed concern about the lack of management tools available at regional level and in particular, the problem of the auditor/client relationship at trust level and the ownership of audit reports which excludes regional scrutiny of audit:

> "The region does not get copies of district audit reports of trusts at a formal level. Mostly I know about financial trouble areas informally but as tools of management the audit report and management letter are missing from the regional kit."
>
> *Regional Director*

The general message from trusts in this study, in particular from senior managers, was that audit was a useful management aid. Occasionally, however, audit findings were not highly rated and seen as a management irritant. One chief executive of a health authority complained that audit had failed to tell them anything they did not already know, which was that the authority was in deep debt. The audit had not helped to solve problems and, according to the chief executive, did not seem to understand the way financial problems can develop and accelerate in the NHS. The chief executive felt strongly that the auditors should have seen at an earlier stage that the authority's strategic spending plans were not realistic and should, at a later audit, have been able to offer strategic solutions to the financial crisis. Given the fiscal plight of the organisation, and its history of mismanagement (it had been subject to a special inquiry), it is not surprising that this particular health authority had nothing positive to say about audit, finding even the negotiated management letter without any constructive suggestions for solving financial problems.

Both finance and general managers in the study had views about the direction and growth of audit in the NHS and the relation between VFM and probity audit for health service organisations. Both internal and external audit have progressed in recent years from what auditors call the 'old tick and bash' system to a more sophisticated operation of checking what is now, in theory, a comprehensive financial management system in the NHS. Finance directors talked about the profound changes that have taken place in audit ideas and methods generally as well as more particularly in the NHS. For example, better financial management is seen as an essential element in performance management and in moving towards a more effective service delivery.

Internal audit has to be right first, however, before an external audit can be effective. And audit is a threshold to quality assurance and value for money in the NHS. At the same time, a regional finance officer expressed concerns about audit becoming absorbed into the management systems of health authorities and trusts and losing its independent role:

> "Planning, policy and performance systems in the NHS have been much more centralised in the last two years. We know that performance management is about delivery of products. Products approved by central government. Internal audit is part of this and big changes are opening up around audit. However, financial management is becoming so much a part of general management and the deeper they get into organisational controls assurance, the less independent they become. Auditors could lose the bog basics of audit, that is looking at items of transaction. We need to move onto systems of financial control but only in addition to the basics of old fashioned audit."
>
> *Financial Director, Health Authority*

As to the appropriate proportions of VFM audit to probity, which currently run at 30% and 70% respectively, all the managers in the study were convinced that probity audit should have priority over VFM audit, in the sense that a VFM audit is no use to an organisation whose financial probity performance is unsatisfactory. An emphasis on probity audit and its improvement is essential to deterring fraud, making it more difficult - if not impossible - in the NHS:

> "It is still the case that if fraudsters are incredibly clever then scandals could happen but by and large the NHS has cleaned up its act. The scandal that happened here took the police three years to prove and the fraud was very sophisticated. It could still happen and that is why we need the assurance of a good probity audit."
>
> *Chief Executive, Hospital Trust*

A chief executive with a strong financial background suggested that a distinction should be drawn between trusts and health authorities when deciding on appropriate proportions of VFM to probity audit. The split of 70%-30% probity to VFM audit is probably about right for trusts, or might sensibly be tipped even further towards probity since their financial transactions are many and complex. On the other hand, health authorities might be better with more VFM audit since their financial transactions are fewer and more straightforward with a greater focus on service strategy and configuration. Furthermore, there are problems with having a common overall audit policy for all health authorities and trusts, given the wide variations in financial skill levels throughout the NHS. Not all trusts, for example, have successfully installed financial management systems. This means that external audit in the NHS is dealing with variable levels of financial competence and development in different trusts.

The final word on the merits and proportions of VFM and probity audits in the NHS came from an experienced director of finance at trust level who thought that the 70%-30% split between probity and VFM audit does not tell the whole story. A few years ago audit was pure probity until the focus changed to VFM. In spite of the proportions remaining in favour of probity, the emphasis in external audit changed to favour VFM. Even in internal audit where the focus is on probity still, auditors are working in a climate of VFM and this has altered audit to the detriment of probity. The finance director recalled the time when this shift in fashion first gripped the imagination of NHS finance officers:

"We took our eye off the probity ball. Even where, as internal auditors, we were supposed to focus mainly on probity. In order for any organisation to flourish it needs a stable financial base. Focusing on the finances of an organisation is a good start to looking at what it is doing. Bad financial organisation paralyses the whole system. Most of the scandals in the NHS which started about fifteen years ago were about poor quality financial control, regional and local, and hospitals and trusts. This was due to several factors. First, financial services in the NHS were neglected in favour of an emphasis on general management. And second, about ten years ago, the audit focus changed to VFM and it was sexy to do VFM rather than probity. Third, around the early 1990s we moved to a 'can do' culture in the NHS arising out of the new management emphasis. Everyone said 'let's be imaginative - let us look at ways of using our resources for better value and get more for our money."

"Then we were stung by the financial tragedies that happened in the early 1990s. The West Midlands, Yorkshire and the South West. All high profile cases. There was a feeling that these cases went much deeper and reflected a malaise in the NHS. But we are, I am pleased to say, moving back in the last five years to a better balance. We have also moved, in this time, to a better financial management. We have had a radical shake-up of internal audit and are moving to a more effective financial control system. It has become sexy to do probity again.

The result is that in the last five years, the NHS aggregated accounts have been unqualified. - that is approved without significant error. The National Audit Office, the official auditor of the NHS as a single financial entity, has found no material errors in the last four years."

Financial Director, Hospital Trust

By a different route, then, this section has come to much the same conclusion as the Audit Commission's own studies of impact. This is that the combination of variability in both the quality of the auditors and in the expectations of the audited makes it impossible to give a single verdict applicable across-the-board. But some conclusions can be drawn from our interviews. First, the Commission's national studies are well-regarded even by those who are highly critical of local auditors. Second, they (like the Commission's own work) identified ways in which audit could be made more useful to the audited, in particular by allowing greater choice of topic. We return to this point in the final section, which examines policy changes and challenges in the increasingly crowded NHS audit arena.

PART 2 - OTHER AUDIT BODIES

2.1 The National Audit Office

Compared to the National Audit Office (NAO), the Audit Commission is a parvenu. The office of Comptroller and Auditor General (C & AG) - the title of the NAO's head, usually a former Permanent Secretary - can be traced back to 1314 (16). The present office of C & AG was created by an Act of Parliament in 1866. Subsequently the NAO itself was created, and its constitutional position and remit clarified by the National Audit Act of 1983. First, the Act entrenched the independence of the C & AG and the NAO from the Executive: the C & AG is an officer of Parliament and is responsible for examining and reporting to the House of Commons on the way in which government spends its money. The NAO must audit and certify the accounts of all government departments. Second, the Act gave statutory recognition - and consequently a higher profile - to the NAO's VFM work. It made explicit what previously had been implicit: that the NAO is responsible for examining the economy, efficiency and effectiveness of government programmes, as well as being the guardian of regularity and probity.

NAO's scope is thus much wider than that of the Audit Commission: its remit covers about £600 billion of public spending or roughly five times the sum which falls under the Commission's umbrella. However, from the perspective of this analysis, the crucial difference between the two bodies lies in their constitutional position. The NAO is an instrument of parliamentary accountability. Its reports prompt and inform the inquiries of the Public Accounts Committee of the House of Committee. There is thus a built-in - politically powerful and highly visible - mechanism for following up NAO's findings. Departmental Accounting Officers - the Permanent Secretary or, in the case of the NHS, the Chief Executive - are subjected to sometimes searching cross-examinations, requiring much preparation. As Peter Hennessy has noted (17): "Whitehall reputations could be made or broken in the PAC. They still can". Which is not to say that NAO criticisms are necessarily accepted or acted upon: Whitehall reputations can be made by mounting a spirited defence or by a subtle strategy of evasion.

In contrast, there is no such national forum for following up the Audit Commission's national VFM studies, even when the recommendations are addressed to the NHS Executive. It has to engineer publicity for its national VFM studies, an enterprise in which it has invested heavily and proved remarkably successful. And the follow up to its national studies is, of course, provided by local auditors, whose findings - as embodied in the management letters - are addressed to a "client", i.e. the health authority or trust, who may not necessarily be receptive or respectful. They are not addressed to a body of professional critics like the members of the Public Accounts Committee. Unsurprisingly, therefore, NHS Executives (or local government ones, for that matter) do not spend much time agonising over their responses to the VFM findings of local auditors - though it may be a different matter if financial regularity or probity is at issue.

In many respects, then, NAO and the Audit Commission are a mirror image of each other. NAO is orientated towards the Whitehall-Westminster axis; the Commission is orientated towards the periphery. The former has a concentrated impact but lacks the means for following up its recommendations at the level of service delivery; the latter has a diffuse impact precisely because it reaches those outer parts of government programmes which NAO cannot. The C & AG has in statute complete freedom to determine which inquiries should be carried out and how; in the case of the Commission its members play an active role in determining its strategy and are, as noted, involved in individual studies. There are clearly defined - and complementary - strengths and weakness as well as roles.

In practice, the contrast is not quite so stark or clear cut. For example, the Public Accounts Committee (and in particular its chairman) exercise a strong influence on the choice of NAO topics. And NAO reports - like those of local auditors - are in many respects negotiated documents. This is apparent from NAO's handbook on how to conduct VFM studies (18). A VFM study begins by consulting the audited body about the methodology and techniques to be used. And it ends by clearing the final report with the department concerned. This often lengthy process involves getting agreement about the "facts", if not necessarily about what implications can be drawn from the facts. Here the advice to auditors is:

> "Unless crucial to an important aspect of a report, it may be better to omit sections of the draft rather than engage in a long drawn out debate and counter argument. Compromise drafts can sometimes confuse the reader."

Lastly, although NAO's principal function is to serve as a parliamentary instrument of accountability, it also has a broader aim. This, to quote the VFM handbook again, is "to help audited bodies improve their performance in achieving VFM". It is in fulfilling this aim that, in the case of the NHS, there is a degree of convergence in the work of NAO and the Commission In what follows, we illustrate this point by looking in summary form at some of NAO's reports in order to pinpoint what is unique about the NAO and where there is a risk of overlap with the Commission.

It is in verifying the national accounts, rather than VFM work, that NAO plays an unchallenged and unique role. Annually, it examines the audited accounts of both the Department of Health and of individual NHS organisations. It does so by "reviewing the work of the auditors appointed by the Audit Commission, scrutinising their reports and findings and ensuring that acceptable quality control policies and procedures existed and operated efficiently"(19). In effect, the report provides a balance sheet of the NHS's financial performance, identifying trusts with serious financial problems. However, the analysis is not concerned with these trusts but with the action taken by the NHS Executive to monitor and remedy the situation. Similarly, the report reviews the extent of fraud in the NHS. Again, the focus is not on individual instances of fraud but on the effectiveness of the strategy followed by the NHS Directorate of Counter-Fraud Services. Overall, then, the emphasis of this annual exercise is very much on the technology of audit and systems of control and the response of the NHS Executive to issues raised by auditors.

The case of the annual review of the accounts points to the difficulty of drawing a neat separation between traditional, financial audit and VFM work. The review would seem to be a pure example of the former. But when it comes to discussing the efficiency and effectiveness of the anti-fraud strategy, it appears to be teetering on the edge of performance audit. The same point applies to a recent report on a topic that has provided the staple of NAO inquiries throughout the existence of the NHS and seen generations of Permanent Secretaries squirming in front of the Public Accounts Committee: the escalating costs of hospital buildings. In analysing the reasons why the cost of a phase in the development of Guy's Hospital rose from an estimate £35.5 million to £160 million, and was completed four years late, the NAO report (20) both identifies the problems encountered and sets out a series of recommendations designed to make the management of such projects more efficient and effective.

Reports on the costs of building hospitals - like the annual certification of the accounts and the occasional inquiries into cases of gross financial mismanagement (21) - are very much a NAO monopoly. Here there is no question of the Audit Commission treading on the NAO's turf or of the NAO duplicating the work of the Commission. And a logical division of labour between the two bodies is indeed possible, as shown by two reports produced in the same year on the same topic: how the NHS buys its supplies. The NAO report (22) concentrated exclusively on the effectiveness and efficiency of the central purchasing body, NHS Supplies. The Commission report (23) dealt exclusively with the management of purchasing in NHS trusts. There was a neat complementarity between the national and the local perspectives of the two exercises.

Time, as well as focus, can prevent duplication. NAO produced a VFM report on fundholding in 1994 (24); the Audit Commission produced a national study a year later (25). Given that fundholding was an evolving experiment, there clearly was good reason to repeat the initial study. This was a case of building on previous work. The methodologies were similar, although the Commission's inquiry was more comprehensive and detailed: whereas the NAO report was based on a sample survey of fundholders, the Commission carried out a national study. So, too, were the main concerns of the two inquiries: the impact of fundholding on services for patients, the effectiveness with which fundholders used their purchasing power and the setting of budgets. On all scores the Commission report was more illuminating than its predecessor, partly because of the greater depth of its research and partly because time had generated more evidence.

So even when the two bodies deal with the same topic, there is scope for differentiation, whether by focus or temporal to avoid the risk of them treading on each other's toes or, more seriously, overloading the audited. However, there are signs of convergence in the style of the two audit organisations, with NAO moving towards the Commission model. The point emerges from two recent reports. The first dealt with hip replacements (26); the second with hospital acquired infections (27). In both cases, there was considerable scope for achieving savings by adopting more effective managerial and clinical policies. In both cases, NAO used an expert panel, backed by a search of the academic literature and visits to the United States in search of good practice models. In both cases there was a survey or census of all hospital trusts, in addition to site visits. In both cases the recommendations are addressed as much to hospital trusts - clinicians as well as managers - as to the Department of Health. In the case of the hip replacement report, trusts were advised that they should consider restricting the prostheses available to consultants to those with long term evidence of effectiveness. In the case of hospital acquired infections, trusts were recommended to improve the system of surveillance and data collection process, while also ensuring the implementation of central advice on handwashing.

In terms of methodology, analysis and target-audience, these two reports were thus quite similar to the kind of studies that the Audit Commission might have produced. And this was reflected in the visual presentation of the reports. Whereas in the past NAO reports were noted for a certain drab austerity, they have now moved nearer the Audit Commission model of using visual devices to punctuate the text. For example, the report on hospital infections even has a whole page figure demonstrating a "simple but effective technique" for washing hands: an illustration presumably not designed for use by members of the Public Accounts Committee but by people working in the NHS. Similarly, like national Audit Commission studies, these two NAO reports illustrate their recommendations by using case studies of good practice drawn from the field: again a reminder that these reports are aimed at an audience beyond the Whitehall-Westminster arena. Indeed NAO sent a copy of the hospital infection report to all Chief Executives and Infection Control Officers.

Convergence does not imply imitation: rather it reflects the fact that audit as an art form adapts to wider changes in government and society. The change in the visual presentation is a case in point: it follows the pattern set by Government White Papers which over the past decade or so have become steadily more populist in design and style on the assumption that they are intended to address not just a policy elite but a wider audience. Other changes in the NAO's approach and methodology can be traced to similar, wider changes. So, for example, NAO started using surveys to gauge public responses to public services much more frequently from the late 1980s onward (28). Similarly, it has begun to use focus groups (29), part of a more general trend towards greater methodological sophistication. At the same time NAO strategy has shifted from concentrating primarily on systems of control to examining substantive issues: the reports on hip replacements and hospital infections are examples of the latter category. In the 1980s more than 80% of NAO's VFM work focussed on systems audit. By the 1990s, this had become very much a minor theme (30).

Like the Audit Commission, NAO faces the problem of constructing the performance which is to be audited: i.e. determining the criteria that are to be used. NAO (unlike the Commission) is explicitly barred from questioning the merits of government policies. But it can, and does, look at whether these have been implemented efficiently and effectively. Which is fine when the goals of government policy are clear: in the case of the hospital infection report, for example, NAO could examine the performance of hospital trusts against departmental guidance. But when there are no such benchmarks against which to assess performance, NAO tends to fall back on much the same rational actor model as the Commission: if adequate data about performance is not collected, if management has no clear policies, if there are unexplained variations (the cost of hip replacements varies from £384 to £7,784), then there is a prima facie case for arguing that the service is not being delivered with adequate efficiency and effectiveness - and that there is scope for saving money. And this is precisely what NAO does: it tends to be keener on claiming that its work actually saves money while the Commission tends to stress service improvements rather more. Thus the Comptroller and Auditor General's latest annual report (31) proudly states:

> "Our work has prompted public bodies to make improvements which have saved the taxpayer nearly £1.2 billion in the past three years, so that we have met our target of saving £7 for every £1 we cost to run. In the light of this, I have raised the target: in future we shall aim to save £8 for every £1 of the Office."

There is a long established machinery for co-ordinating the activities of NAO and the Audit Commission, with regular meetings to discuss the work programme in order to avoid duplication or collision. Similarly, there are frequent cross-memberships on advisory and expert groups and very occasionally officials even participate in each other's studies. It is not clear, however, how far the spirit of co-operation goes (32). For the spirit of competition is also strong. In the words of one NAO official, 'We tend to see them as upstarts. They see us as dinosaurs." And while the machinery appears to succeed in avoiding overt duplication, convergence does create a paradox. This is why while the Audit Commission's mission is in the field of service delivery, some of its most successful and admired work has been in the national studies that shape work at the periphery. And while it has a field force for carrying out its missionary work, it has no institutionalised forum for its national studies and no mechanism for feeding back the results of its local work into the national policy process. Conversely, NAO's most successful and admired work is addressed to national policy makers - in Parliament and in the departments - but it has no mechanism for following up its recommendations as to responsibility for service delivery in the NHS and elsewhere, though the latter appears to be becoming increasingly important. We return to this point in Part 3, which examines wider policy issues and options.

2.2 Joint Reviews of Social Services

Joint Reviews of the Social Services Inspectorate and the Audit Commission were set up in the early 1990s in response to government, civil service and academic disquiet about the effectiveness of SSI monitoring of social services departments. In 1996 the Audit Miscellaneous Provisions Act set out the division of labour and resources between the Department of Health and the Audit Commission whereby the Department had funding responsibilities and the Commission had overall operational responsibilities (including engaging with SSI). Joint reviewing was intended to provide an independent assessment of how well the public is being served by social services in each local authority in England and Wales. Negotiations between all interested parties resulted in a mixture of VFM audit and inspection becoming the Joint Review System with self-styled reviewers, rejecting the label of auditors or inspectors, carrying out the reviews.

The path of Joint Reviewing did not, however, always run smooth. Initially, the number of reviews produced fell short of the Department's expectations. The result was tension between the Department and the Directorate, the former claiming operational inefficiency and the latter disputing targets and claiming under-funding. All disputes were eventually resolved by an increase in Departmental funding. To add to the complications, work on reviews began with no firm details having been worked out on the funding and timing of them and, furthermore, with little attention paid to the business management process of running the organisation.

The division of managerial and operational responsibilities between the Audit Commission and the Social Services Inspectorate are also not without tensions. At the managerial level of the Reviews, joint activity begins and ends at Assistant Secretary level in the SSI and at Assistant Director level in the Commission. There is effectively no joint working between the Department and the Commission at the reviewing level since reviewers, although supposed to have a mix of skills, are recruited mainly from local government rather than from the Audit Commission.

But, if the Joint Review struggled with operational weaknesses, it fared better in its pursuit of an up-dated regulatory methodology. The systems and tools of Review are surprisingly robust and the Directorate has emerged, with hindsight, as the forerunner of the more recent Best Value Inspectorate (Box 6, p:105). For example, one notion of the Review is that good social services require well run councils and an essential part of the Review system involves, therefore, scrutinising the managerial capacity of the local authority as a whole. The overall conclusions of the reports of Joint Review of Social Services Departments start with authority wide assessments. Examples below from two London Boroughs illustrate the review technique:

> "The Review Team concludes that overall the authority is in a strong position to achieve its own objectives of excellence and efficiency in the delivery of social services. Southwark Council has invested in the staff it employs, in its partnerships with others and in its information systems so that users in high need receive timely and flexible services" (33).
>
> *Southwark London Borough Council Review*

"The Review Team concludes that overall the needs of the people in Barking and Dagenham are not well met. Many people receive services but they are so thinly spread that quality is poor. The Authority's track record in implementing change is not auspicious and it faces major challenges in addressing the issues highlighted in this report. Progress will require the combined resources of the whole council" (34).

Barking and Dagenham London Borough Council Review

The Best Value inspection is similarly informed by notions of authority wide performance. Furthermore, the focus of both review and inspection is broad rather than deep, with an emphasis on management - corporate and departmental - and the use of resources. Professional judgement is also reviewed but is considered and assessed within the wider context of service provision. Joint Review of Social Services, in particular, set out to avoid appearing to be steeped in professional concerns. Both Review and Inspection have a bottom-up and user and, in the case of the Review, carer focus. The aims, principles and performance criteria of Review, as set out in Box 5, are also evident in Best Value.

Box 5 Joint Review Strategy

Aims
- To improve services for individuals
- To enable authorities to shape better services
- To promote better standards and improve the management of practice
- To secure better value for money

Principles
- User focus for services
- Partnership between users, carers and providers
- Inclusion of all stakeholders in social services through reviews
- Evidence based practices for services
- Consistency of reviews
- Corporacy approach of reviews - looking at performance of whole authority as well as social services
- Development approach of reviews - enable every authority to improve its performance
- Openness of reviews - publishing review methodology, reports on individual authorities and annual reports on Joint Review

Performance Criteria
- Are services focused on meeting individuals' needs?
- Can the authority shape better services for the future?
- Is performance effectively managed?
- Are resources managed to maximise value for money and quality?

Joint Review Guide

The construction and execution of Joint Reviews accurately reflect the aims and principles, as well as the refined and revised methodology referred to above. Fieldwork begins at the 'bottom' with surveys of users and carers and works its way up to corporate management interviews with Directors of Social Services Departments and Chief Executives of local authorities. Then Chairmen and Members of the authority are interviewed or surveyed. All questionnaires, case studies and interviews have a user/carer focus and are based on a framework as follows:

1- the individual needs of clients and the wider population.
2- the way services are shaped.
3- the way resources are managed.
4- the way the performance of the service is managed.

Other report findings reflect the operational style of the Review framework. For example, the Cornwall Review which concluded that overall the people of Cornwall are well served by their social services, in addition, emphasised both the positive views of users surveyed and the efficiency of service delivery:

> "The authority maintains a strong focus on controlling costs of services, adequate systems for ensuring the quality of services and a capacity to make changes when necessary. The arrangements for obtaining services for adult users strongly support user choice" (36).
>
> *Cornwall County Council Review*

This report also pointed out, however, the wider constraints under which the authority was operating and its less than satisfactory collaboration with other service providers:

> "Demographic trends and financial pressures are challenging the capacity of social services where health and social services is vital. The Review found evidence of

effective collaboration by operational staff. A number of people in Cornwall told the Review Team that they considered the antipathy between the Cornwall and Isles of Scilly Authority and Cornwall's Social Services to be deeply damaging to services. The Joint Review Team supports this view and considers that, over time, these difficulties, if not resolved, will erode the Authority's overall ability to serve its population well."

Cornwall County Council Review

In an authority which was given an overall low performance rating for its social services, the Review criticised, in particular, its poor management and use of resources:

"The authority has failed to tackle fundamental management questions, notably the essential requirement to match resource strategy (for example, allocation of funds) with its policies and to ensure that policy is implemented effectively. The Authority spends more per head of population on social services than similar authorities but does not target resources at achieving specific policy objectives" (37).

Barking and Dagenham London Borough Council Review

Management of resources, and co-ordination and collaboration with other service providers dominate many report findings while professional issues get a lesser scrutiny from the review team. In one authority with an overall low performance rating, however, criticisms of professional staff performance were part of the Review, although these were contained within an overall management and resource assessment:

"People in Coventry are not consistently well served. While there are some gems of quality and innovation, the choices that have been made in resourcing and managing the Department leave some vulnerable people at risk. In particular, there are serious problems with childcare. In January 1998 there were 301 child protection investigations and 56 children on the child protection register who did not have an allocated worker" (38).

Coventry City Council Review

What the Joint Review claims not to do is look at performance against a prescribed set of standards. And what they also claim not to do is to confront departments and local authorities with their service shortcomings. The Joint Review style was described thus:

"Our approach is contextual and consultative. We look at the internal dynamics of social services departments and the local context and history of the local authority i.e population, geography and industry. We also look at the future capacity of the department and calculate its projected direction - using an historical perspective. We then emphasise the consultative nature of the review process. We are never, except in very extreme circumstances, confrontational. The review process emphasises the development of the local authority as well as the stewardship and accountability for the use of public money. The Social Services Departments are helped to see themselves and develop the means to review their own operation and organisation. We take the view that local authorities need to know themselves in order to run their services effectively. We regard self-review information as essential management information for the authority."

Joint Review Manager

Although the progress of Joint Reviews has been slower than the Department of Health anticipated, it is expected that in time all Social Services Departments will have been reviewed. No authority can refuse to be reviewed; neither can any ask for a delay or reprieve. All local authorities being reviewed are expected to supply the reviewers with base information about themselves and their service provision before the review starts.

The complete review from set up to final report takes about one year although the fieldwork and analysis takes thirty days approximately and consultation and feedback takes another sixty days. All in all, the review itself is a ninety day job, during which time it will be subject to some modifications by consultees. The Joint Review documents are open and public but the primary audiences are chairmen of Social Services Departments. The reviewers can suggest reforms to departments and authorities but cannot force change. It is the elected members who are expected to follow up review criticisms and engineer changes. The Reviews are followed up by audits and SSI inspections, both of which will have seen the reviews.

2.3 The Commission for Health Improvement

Both NAO and the Audit Commission have their origins in a concern that public money should be properly and well spent. They are instruments of fiscal accountability. The origins of the Commission for Health Improvement (CHI), created by the 1999 Health Act, are very different. They reflect a concern about clinical standards. The Commission is to audit the quality of care in the NHS. It has three main functions. It will review the implementation and adequacy of clinical governance: all trusts will be visited every four years and those deemed to be performing poorly will be visited more frequently. Second, it will monitor the implementation of national service frameworks. Third, it will carry out special inquiries for the Secretary of State.

Like the Audit Commission, CHI is an independent non-departmental public body. Like the Audit Commission, CHI's members are nominated by the Secretary of State. But though independent in status, CHI is very much the instrument of the Secretary of State: in effect, if not in name, an inspectorate for the NHS. Its budget is determined by the Department of Health. So, too, are the main elements of its programme of work, such as the special inquiries. As the 1999 Act unambiguously states: "The Secretary of State may give directions with respect to the exercise of any functions of the Commission" and "the Commission must comply with any directions". If in practice the relationship is not as brutally one-sided as this wording might suggest, it is nevertheless clear where ultimate authority rests. CHI is thus, functionally if not constitutionally, a rather different animal from either NAO or the Audit Commission.

But invoking the notion of quality does not of itself define a unique role for CHI, clearly demarcating its sphere of competence and action. For, as we have seen, the VFM work of both the Audit Commission and NAO has increasingly encompassed the quality dimension: indeed logically quality issues and effectiveness would seem to be inextricably linked (could a low-quality service be effective?). So, for example, both the Audit Commission's 1995 study of services for elderly patients with hip fracture and NAO's recent report on hip replacements explicitly dealt with the quality of care delivered to patients. Indeed, in Opposition Labour had flirted with the idea of transforming the Audit Commission into a Quality Commission. The distinguishing characteristic of CHI is therefore to be found in its inspectorial role: in the fact that it will regularly review the performance of service deliverers In this respect its role is best compared to the annual audit of the accounts rather than the more sporadic VFM work of local auditors. The quadrennial reviews of the clinical governance systems will be the equivalent of the auditors' checks on the financial control systems of trusts. While the VFM work of the Audit Commission and NAO from time to time illuminates specific services, CHI will report on quality control systems and service delivery as a whole. In doing so it will direct the searchlight of audit and publicity at specific institutions.

CHI is still in the process of inventing itself, so it is much too early to judge how it will carry out its tasks. However, the main elements of its strategy have already been laid out (39). Reviews will be preceded and informed by an assessment drawing on clinical indicators, reports and inspections carried out by external bodies such as the Royal Colleges as well as patients' diaries recording their experience of using services. The reviews will be carried out by teams of five - consisting of a doctor, a nurse, a therapist, a manager and lay person - and usually last for five days. The emphasis will be very much on a "developmental and supportive rather than confrontational" style (which is why CHI, in contrast to Ministers, rejects the inspectorial label). A report, and an agreed programme of action, will be published after the visit.

So CHI's style will be very different from that of either NAO or the Audit Commission. It will mainly rely on part time reviewers rather than career inspectors. Their authority will thus be based on their professional backgrounds rather than on their experience of, or specialised skills in, auditing: the reverse of the balance of competencies in the other two audit organisations. In this respect, as well as in its repudiation of the inspectorial label, CHI is the direct descendant of the 1970s Hospital Advisory Service (40). And it remains to be seen what happens if the professional construction of "good performance" differs from the way it is defined and perceived by users. Most important of all, perhaps, CHI reports - in strong contrast to those of local auditors - will feed directly into the Department of Health's management processes. They will, in effect, be managerial prompts and tools for the Department's regional offices. It is these which will be responsible for ensuring the implementation of the action plans agreed during the visits. While the client of NAO is Parliament and that of local audit is the audited body, CHI's client is the Department of Health: a potential source of tension, given CHI's desire to play a "developmental and supportive" role.

But even though CHI is performing - in many respects - a different function from either NAO or the Audit Commission, there remains the possibility of both overlap and overload. The Audit Commission has, as we have seen, always regarded issues of governance as part of its brief. Thus local auditors invariably examine managerial and organisational structures and processes as part of their annual exercise. It would be difficult, and probably undesirable, to exclude clinical governance from this surveillance. At the same time CHI's arrival on the scene is a net addition to the audit burden. While five days every four years may not seem an inordinate burden, the process of preparing for the inspection tends to be a multiple of the length of the visit (although it may be argued that there are benefits as well as costs for the audited organisation since an impending visit provides an incentive to polish up the organisation and that, further, the preparation costs diminish after the first visit).

In the event, the Audit Commission and CHI have agreed on a "memorandum of understanding" setting out the terms of their co-operation (41). This provides for the co-ordination of CHI's clinical governance inspections and the Commission's audit of the management of organisations, as well as for collaborative exercises: thus CHI's first review of the implementation of national service frameworks, that for cancer, is being carried out by a joint team. In this respect, the Audit Commission can build on precedent: the joint inspection of social services that it carries out in collaboration with the Social Services Inspectorate, which are concerned both with the efficient and effective use of resources and quality.

However, questions about the spheres of activity of the different audit agencies and inspectorates, as well as about the links between them, are likely to continue to climb up the policy agenda. The Government's emphasis on promoting cross-cutting policies - and joint working in their delivery (42) - has implications both for the individual strategies of the audit agencies and for the relationship between them: a point we explore further in the next, concluding, part of this study.

PART 3 - CONCLUSIONS AND POLICY ISSUES

3.1 A challenging environment

In concluding this study, we draw out the implications of our findings and identify policy issues that remain to be resolved. Two points, however, need to be stressed by way of preface: the twin achievements of the Audit Commission that risk being overlooked because taken for granted. First, over the past decade the Audit Commission has directed a powerful searchlight on the NHS. The succession of VFM national studies analysed in Part 1 has provided a series of snapshots of the NHS at work. When these snapshots are put together, they provide a unique portrait of the NHS: they have illuminated, among other things, the information poverty of the service, the seemingly haphazard patterns of staff deployment and the lack of explicit and coherent policies in trusts. If the NHS has been perceived as starved of resources, it is therefore at least in part because of the way in which those resources have been used: the fact that the Audit Commission has always been able to find exemplars of good practice suggests that the capacity to deliver good quality services, holding budgetary constraints constant, is very unequally distributed. Improving that capacity may therefore be as important as increasing the budget. No other body, and certainly not the academic community, can match the Commission's record of providing such a flow of information. If accountability is, among other things, about transparency and visibility, then the Commission has stripped a lot of veils from the NHS.

Second, it is impossible to over-stress the importance of the least visible part of the Audit Commission's activities: the 70 % of time spent by local auditors on inspecting the accounts of health authorities and trusts, monitoring the systems of financial control and reviewing the procedures for identifying risk and preventing fraud. The fact that this aspect of the Commission's work only rarely hits the headlines - that financial scandals or melt-downs are surprisingly rare in the NHS - is, of itself, a tribute to the effectiveness of the audit system, although the credit for better systems of accounting must be shared with governmental bodies, in particular the Treasury and the NHS Executive. There is now much emphasis on improving management and financial control, as well as rushing to the rescue of trusts which might otherwise cause political embarrassment to the government of the day by going bankrupt. In what follows, we shall not discuss the Audit Commission's role as the guardian of regularity, sound financial management and probity in the NHS any further. Here we simply note, and emphasise, that detection and prevention of fraud and fiscal incompetence are the Commission's indispensable core function. It is a function that is, if anything, likely to become still more important as the flow of money to individual trusts becomes more complex, with some of the cash coming from the new Performance Fund and new hybrid agencies like Health Action Zones spring up.

The other point to note, before addressing specific issues, is that the Audit Commission is in the process of adapting itself to the changes in the institutional and political environment in which it operates. Many of those changes, like the creation of CHI and the government's emphasis on joined-up or "seamless" service delivery, have already been noted. Others include the National Institute for Clinical Excellence (NICE), which is charged with producing precisely the kind of models of good practice and service configuration that auditors require as benchmarks against which to assess performance, and the Department of Health's expanded battery of performance indicators which will be used to rank health authorities and trusts. Wider constitutional innovations - the creation of a National Assembly for Wales and a Greater London Authority - have further changed the environment in which the Commission works.

The Audit Commission has responded to these changes, and other pressures, in a variety of ways (43-44). Here we simply summarise the main changes, exploring some of their implications in greater detail below. First, the Commission's cross-sectoral approach will be extended and developed. Second, better methods of assessing and reporting on the financial standing of NHS bodies are to be introduced. Third, VFM work in the NHS will be more closely aligned with the NHS Executive's priorities and those of local bodies. Fourth, there is to be more emphasis on citizen and user perspectives in evaluating services. Fifth, there will be a commitment to identifying what works and helping to spread innovation and good practice. Finally, the Commission has launched a "best value inspectorate" for local government (Box 6) which may eventually have knock-on effects on the NHS.

Box 6 The best value inspectorate

The best value inspectorate, established by the 1999 Local Government Act, replaces the previous compulsory competitive tendering regime. It is intended to improve democratic accountability by putting an obligation on local authorities to demonstrate to local people that they are achieving continuous improvements in all their services. To do so, local authorities will be required to review all of their services every five years. In doing so, they will be expected to demonstrate that they "have applied the 4Cs of best value to every review". The 4Cs are:

- Challenging why and how a service is being provided
- Comparing their performance with that of others
- Embracing fair competition as a means of securing efficient and effective services
- Consulting with local taxpayers, customers and the wider business community

The Audit Commission's inspectors will test the extent to which the reviews of local authorities meet these criteria. They will further carry out "reality checks" by looking not only at the extent to which local services meet national standards, where these exist, but at the perceptions of users. They will also carry out brief observational studies of the services. The services will then be ranked on a scale of 0 to 3 stars. Each inspection will produce recommendations for improvements, drawing on the Commission's national experience. The aim is to "learn from what works".

If a local authority fails to respond to the findings of the inspectorate, the Audit Commission may refer it to the Secretary of State. The Secretary of State has a variety of powers under the 1999 Act, including the power to transfer an authority's responsibilities to another authority or third party.

Source: Best Value Inspection Service *Seeing is believing: how the Audit Commission will carry out its best value inspections in England*. London: Audit Commission 2000

In our study we are therefore reporting on a rapidly evolving situation, in which the effectiveness of new initiatives, new institutions and new policies remains to be tested. Given this uncertainty, a degree of caution in making predictions and putting forward recommendations is advisable.

3.2 Joined-up government and joined-up audit

Two quite different, if related, issues arise. The first is how to audit services which involve integrating (or at least co-ordinating) the activities of two or more programmes each of which will have its own line of accountability. The second is how to integrate (or at least co-ordinate) the activities of two or more audit agencies, each of which will have a distinct constitutional and institutional history. The two issues are related in those cases where different lines of accountability bring different audit agencies into play. (Here we use the concept of "audit" in a broad, non-technical sense to encompass also those inspectorates which examine the performance, though not necessarily the financial accounts, of publicly funded programmes.)

In auditing or inspecting programmes that involve co-ordinating the activities of NHS and local authority services, the Audit Commission starts from a position of strength in the increasingly competitive audit market. Here is a niche in the market where the Commission has a unique selling point: its experience of working across both the NHS and local government. Further, it can cite its collaboration with CHI, although as one Commission official remarked: "We do all the work and they take all the credit". Not surprisingly, therefore, it has embraced the notion with enthusiasm.

"The Commission is uniquely placed to help local bodies as they implement multi-agency solutions to the delivery of important services", in the words of the Commission's chair (45): "We have a strong track record in undertaking studies that cut across boundaries, whether organisational, professional or geographical " Accordingly, the Commission is appointing auditors who will be responsible, in particular geographical areas, for work on programmes that cut across health authorities, trusts and local authorities: mental health for older people and rehabilitation services in the first instance. These are special appointments, in addition to the existing auditors responsible for individual trusts and authorities. This, clearly, is a promising initiative, although it remains to be seen how the audited bodies will react to cross-cutting recommendations that may threaten the autonomy of their own services.

To make this last point is to raise a wider issue with relevance to collaboration between both service delivering agencies and inspectorates. The excited rhetoric of joined up government, the launch of multiple initiatives designed to engage different agencies in common enterprises, appears to reflect the belief that something that is so obviously rational and desirable must also be unproblematic. History suggests otherwise: the joint approach to social policy of the 1970s, also launched on a wave of enthusiasm, ended in disillusion. The experience carries a number of warnings for the present (46). To a large degree cross-cutting work is an unnatural activity. Organisations and professions have their own routines, cultures and languages. In requiring people to learn new routines, new cultures and new languages, it imposes heavy costs on both organisations and individuals. The potential gains from collaboration therefore have to compete with such enduring organisational imperatives as protecting budgets, maintaining autonomy and professional self-interest. A new structure of incentives may therefore be required to change organisational routines and promote co-operation.

The Audit Commission has such an incentive, for the reasons given above: that, in a competitive situation, it sees itself as being uniquely well placed to exploit the new emphasis of public policy - as well as an opportunity to regain some the ground that may be lost to CHI. Hence the stress on its record of collaboration with other inspectorates, such as OFSTED. The National Audit Office, too, has adapted to the joined-up government theme: for example, it has carried out a study of obesity, a topic which involves a variety of agencies. But a willingness to engage in joined-up inspection cannot be taken for granted: the prospect may be a threat to some, just as it is an opportunity for others. The case of the joint review of social services is a case in point. It is now a successful model of collaboration between the Audit Commission and the Department of Health's Social Service Inspectorate. But there were problems, as we have seen, in the early days. And there are hints of lingering resentment within the SSI at being forced into this marriage and the implied criticism of its own role: while the Audit Commission gave our research every possible help, the DoH Chief Inspector vetoed access to the joint review process.

Given that individual auditors and inspectors have their own organisational imperatives and given therefore that effective co-operation cannot be taken for granted, there seems to be a case for a systematic audit of audit: i.e. monitoring over time the evolving relationship between the different auditors and inspectors, examining whether they tread on each other's turf and reviewing their cumulative impact on the audited. It is unlikely that the Public Audit Forum can play such a role; it was set up to provide a focus for developmental thinking about public audit, not to act as an independent observer. Similarly, it is not clear that the Cabinet Office's Performance and Innovation Unit is equipped for such a long-term task. Further, sponsorship of the various audit bodies is fragmented among many Whitehall departments, while NAO is accountable only to Parliament. Creating a new supervisory auditor would almost certainly be an excessively heavy-handed way of addressing this problem. Ensuring regular systematic cross-auditor reviews, say every five years, might be more appropriate.

3.3 Who defines performance and how?

One of the themes of this report has been that the art and skill of auditors lies largely - particularly though not exclusively when carrying out VFM work - in constructing the performance which is to be audited and devising tools of judgment. Here it is worth noting two developments likely to affect the way in which they carry out this task. Both have already been touched on previously but both deserve further elaboration, particularly because they may in practice pull against each other. The first is the creation of a new standard-setting institution in the NHS. The second is the increasing emphasis, common to the Audit Commission, CHI and the best quality inspectorate, on using consumer perceptions as a currency of evaluation.

The creation of the National Institute of Clinical Excellence promises, as noted above, to generate standards of practice against which performance can be assessed. Much of this will, of course, be more relevant to CHI than to the Audit Commission. Similarly, national service frameworks will provide models of appropriate service configuration. So, to an extent at least, auditors will increasingly be able to draw on evidence based criteria for making their judgments, although it seems highly likely that (as always) evidence will often speak with two or more voices and that much will be left to interpretative discretion. Still, these developments appear to represent at least a first step towards creating a technocratic basis for audit.

Contrariwise, the emphasis on using the consumer perspective - a trend common to all audit bodies - may pull in the opposite direction. We cannot assume that citizens and users will use the same criteria as the technical experts in judging what is a good performance. If that were so, there would be no reason to invest in consulting them. It may be that (to turn a phrase of Bevan's on its head) users prefer to run a higher risk of dying in a well-swept and well furnished hospital, attended by loving but poorly qualified staff and with a television set and telephone on their bedside table than to have better chances of survival in a spartan hospital where the excellent but stressed staff are brisk if not curt. The point, of course, is that there are different dimensions of performance. And the question for auditors will be what weight to give to the different perspectives.

The emphasis on the consumer perspective also raises questions about efficiency and effectiveness. The NHS Plan (47) provides that all NHS Trusts "will have to ask patients and carers for their views on the services they have received", as well as giving all patients leaving hospital "the opportunity to record their views about the standards of care they have received". This is on top of the large scale national surveys commissioned by the Department of Health. If, in addition, auditors and inspectors are to carry out their own surveys, there may be a long-term risk of a new iatrogenic complaint in the NHS: survey fatigue among patients. Given the costs involved it might be sensible for the parties involved, auditors, inspectors and NHS bodies, to agree on a standard model for consulting users and citizens so that a single set of data would be acceptable to all of them.

There is a further problem to consider when seeking to incorporate the user perspective into the construction and assessment of performance. As we have seen, the Audit Commission in particular has sought to include consumers in the advisory groups that help to develop the criteria of assessment. But who should speak for the consumer? In the case of diabetes services, a long standing condition which does not, however, incapacitate those suffering from it, there was no problem in finding people who could speak from their own experience (though there was no guarantee that they were "representative", in the strict statistical sense). But it is not at all self-evident who can best speak for the survivors, a minority anyway, of critical care: are relatives an adequate substitute? Inevitably, therefore, reliance tends to be placed on organised activists, i.e. those speaking on behalf of pressure groups. Again, their representativeness cannot be taken for granted. There is no obvious solution to this puzzle. But the fact that there is a puzzle should be born in mind whenever the notion of incorporating the consumer perspective in audit is invoked. The prescription offers not a solution but a challenge.

3.4 Improving the effectiveness of audit

In considering its strategy for the future, the Audit Commission faced a paradox. The Commission, as noted at the beginning, prides itself on its independent status, its ability to act as "a fearless independent commentator". Unlike the various inspectorates and CHI, it is self financed. Unlike NAO, it is not inhibited in principle about criticising government policy. Its national studies frequently raise issues that governments might well prefer to avoid. But, as our analysis suggests, there is a price to be paid for this independence. It is that the Commission's VFM work may fail to engage with the dynamics of the NHS, despite the consultations that precede the launch of individual studies. If the evidence about the impact of VFM activities - in terms of changing practice in the NHS - is at best ambiguous, one reason may be that they are often seen as a distraction from more urgent national and local priorities. The Commission's success in putting new issues on the agenda may, in fact, be seen as an irritant: a distraction from more immediately pressing, because politically visible, business.

In the event, the Commission's strategy for the coming few years (48) will tilt the balance more towards integrating its programme of work with the agenda of the NHS. In selecting topics for national VFM studies account will be taken of national NHS priorities and the studies themselves will be slimmer documents. At the same time a different strategy is being developed for the VFM studies carried out by local auditors. The Audit Commission is to develop a "portfolio" of VFM topics, from which trusts and auditors can then select those which are most appropriate to local circumstances: i.e. where, in the light of comparative data and a preliminary diagnostic inquiry, service improvements are most needed. The first four VFM reviews for the portfolio - day surgery, catering, accident and emergency services and ward nursing - are now being developed; the portfolio will be expanded in future years. Auditors who are specialists in the subject will carry out the work.

This strategy certainly meets many of the criticisms encountered in our interviews with managers in the NHS and builds bridges between the Audit Commission and the NHS Executive. It should make NHS trusts more receptive to the intervention of auditors, in so far as these will be seen to be responding to local perceptions of problems rather than imposing their own. It also carries some risks, of course: notably, that auditors may become over-anxious to sell their services to the audited, so compromising their independence. Whether or not the result will be to increase the impact of the VFM work - in terms of promoting changes in governance and practice - remains to be seen: the Audit Commission proposes to invest in research into how change happens in the NHS and the characteristics of successful VFM reviews. The difficulty of attributing specific changes to the intervention of auditors - of insulating their contribution from all the other factors involved - may, however, make it hard to draw any quantifiable conclusions. Auditors may well be able to play a role as the midwives of change; they are not likely to be in a position to claim parentage.

But there is another worry. This is that the Audit Commission may have chosen the wrong currency of evaluation for judging its own performance. How far should it be the role of auditors or inspectors to promote change? Should their effectiveness be assessed in terms of the impact on organisation and activity? Should they even be considered as the midwives of change? The questions need to be asked because - like the emphasis on the consumer perspective - this particular definition of good performance has become part of the conventional wisdom without much challenge. Everyone in the field - NAO, CHI and the rest - now appear to be competing to measure their effectiveness in these terms. But here, surely, there is a need to distinguish between two very distinct activities. First, there is the process of identifying weaknesses (whether in the use of resources or in the governance structure) and making recommendations for change. Second, there is the process of working with the organisation concerned to make the necessary improvements. It is not self-evident that the latter, management-consultancy type of activity is most appropriately carried out by auditors, although it may well be the determining factor in bringing about actual change.

If success in acting as a change agent in the NHS becomes accepted as the criterion of success for audit, the result may be to distort its activities and divert it from its fundamental purpose. If, on the other hand, we start by returning to the traditional notion of audit as the servant of accountability (49), then it is possible to define the "impact" of audit in a very different way. Instead of asking for evidence of change in the NHS as a result of audit activities, we should be asking about evidence about the effectiveness of audit institutions in making the activities of publicly funded services and programmes transparent and meshing with the institutional machinery of accountability.

At the national level the Audit Commission has, as suggested earlier, been successful in giving transparency to the activities of the NHS, even though its searchlight tends to flicker erratically rather than systematically. But, in contrast to the National Audit Office, there has been no linkage with the parliamentary system of accountability. There is no machinery for following up its national studies, even though many of their recommendations are addressed to the NHS Executive. Yet, potentially, there is a client: the House of Commons Health Committee. The Committee at present relies on part-time advisers, hired for particular inquiries. The result is that the varying quality of these advisers is reflected in the varying quality of the Committee's reports. In principle the Committee can draw on NAO reports if the Public Accounts Committee gives clearance. In practice, this happens very rarely. Matching the Commission and the Committee would thus seem to be in the interest of both. It would give the Commission a national platform and it would give the Committee an instrument of inquiry.

At the local level, the Audit Commission's record is less impressive, if only because of a certain ambiguity about its role and audience. In the case of financial audit, the role is clear cut: auditors must ensure regularity and probity and sound the alarm if the trust is heading towards financial bankruptcy. In the case of VFM audit, to reiterate one of our main themes, the notion of "good performance" is much more elusive. In the former case, audit is emphatically the guardian of the public interest. In the latter case, audit appears to be addressing the client organisation as much as the wider public. This is reflected in the management letters. Although available to the public, management letters are addressed to the board of the health authority or trust concerned, not to the public. In cases of fraud or poor financial control, these letters tend to be reasonably clear in presenting their conclusions. Otherwise they tend to be couched in a cautious language which needs considerable decoding before their inner meaning emerges. Local auditors are not in the veil stripping business.

In terms of giving transparency to the operations of the NHS at the local level, the Audit Commission is therefore not effective at present (and the Commission may well consider that this neither is, nor should be, its function). However, its over-diplomatic style may be thrown into greater relief if CHI and the best value inspectorate produce more informative reports. In any case, the Commission already has an in-house model of how to produce reports that are designed to illuminate all aspects of local service provision: the reports of the joint reviews of social services which examine organisational strengths and weaknesses, as well as the quality of service delivery. The case for moving in this direction is further strengthened by the fact that the Government's NHS Plan has created an opening for creating a link between the Audit Commission and the political institutions of the local community. Local authorities are to have the power to scrutinise the NHS in their area: a new (if somewhat weak) line of accountability. The reports of local auditors could have an important role in supporting such scrutinies

It would be foolhardy to claim that giving greater visibility to the activities, both national and local, of the Audit Commission would, in itself, translate into accelerated change in the NHS. Similarly, t would be rash to argue that meshing those activities with representative institutions, both national and local, would have such an effect. All we would claim is that, in terms of strengthening the instruments of accountability, they are desirable in themselves, and as by-products, might conceivably give extra impetus to the drive towards greater economy, efficiency and effectiveness in the NHS.

REFERENCES

1. Christopher D. Foster and Francis J. Plowden *The State under Stress* Buckingham: Open University Press 1996

2. E.L. Normanton *The Accountability & Audit of Government* Manchester: Manchester University Press 1966

3. Michael Power *The Audit Society: Rituals of Verification* Oxford: Oxford University Press 1997

4. Sir David Cooksey *"Chairman's Foreword"* in *Audit Commission Annual Report and Accounts, 1995* London: Audit Commission 1995

5. Audit Commission *Annual Report, 1998* London: Audit Commission 1998

6. Audit Commission *Annual Reports, 1996 & 1997* London: Audit Commission 1996 & 1997

7. Jennifer Dixon and Rudolf Klein It's all in the balance *Health Service Journal* Vol.107 June 1997 26-27

8. As first suggested by Patricia Day and Rudolf Klein *Inspecting the Inspectorates* York: Joseph Rowntree Memorial Trust 1990

9. Anita Houghton *Results of the study selection consultation exercise* Audit Commission internal document 19 October 1998

10. Jo Garcia, Maggie Renshaw, Berverley Fitzsimons, Janet Keene *First class delivery: A national survey of women's views of maternity care* London: Audit Commission 1998

11. Audit Commission *An Inspector Calls: Quality Review Programme for Auditors* London: Audit Commission 1994

12. Audit Commission *Review of the Audit Commission's Quality Control Regime* London: Audit Commission 1999. Mimeo.

13. Neil Carter, Rudolf Klein and Patricia Day *How organisations measure success: the use of performance indicators in government* London: Routledge 1992

14. Audit Commission *Audit effectiveness review* London: Audit Commission 1997. Mimeo.

15. Audit Commission *What is the impact of the Audit Commission's Value for Money work?* London: Audit Commission 1999

16. National Audit Office *The role of the NAO* London: NAO no date

17. Peter Hennessy *Whitehall* London: Fontana 1989

18. National Audit Office *Value for money: handbook* London: NAO 1997

19. Comptroller and Auditor General Office *NHS (England) Summarised Accounts, 1998-99* London: The Stationery Office 2000 HC 356

20. Comptroller and Auditor General *Cost Over-runs, Funding problems and Delays on Guy's Hospital Phase 111 Development* London: The Stationery office HC 761

21. Committee of Public Accounts *West Midlands Regional Health Authority: Regionally managed services organisation*

57th. Report Session 1992-1993 London: HMSO 1993 HC 485

22. Comptroller and Auditor General *National Health Service Supplies in England* London: HMSO 1996 HC 457

23. Audit Commission *Goods for Your Health: Improving Supplies Management in NHS Trusts* London: Audit Commission 1996

24. National Audit Office *General Practice Fundholding in England* London: HMSO 1995

25. Audit Commission *What the Doctor Ordered: A study of GP Fundholders in England and Wales* London: HMSO 1996

26. Comptroller and Auditor General *Hip replacements: getting it right first time* London: The Stationery Office 2000 HC 417

27. Comptroller and Auditor General *The Management and Control of Hospital Acquired Infection in Acute NHS Trusts in England* London:The Stationery Office 2000 HC 230

28. Christopher Pollitt, Xavier Girre, Jeremy Lonsdale, Robert Mul, Hilkka Summa and Marit Waerness *Performance or Compliance? Performance audit and public management in five countries* Oxford: Oxford University Press 1999

29. National Audit Office *Focus groups: How to apply the technique to VFM work* London: NAO 1997

30. Pollitt *et al op.cit.*

31. Comptroller and Auditor General *Helping the nation spend wisely: annual report, 1999* London: NAO 1999

32. Mary Bowerman The National Audit Office and the Audit Commission: Co-operation in areas where their VFM responsibilities interface *Financial Accountability & Management* Vol.10 No.1 1994 pp. 47-63

33. Joint Reviews of Local Authorities' Social Services *A Report of the Review of Social Services in Southwark London Borough Council* London: Audit Commission 1997.

34. Joint Reviews of Local Authorities' Social Services *A Report of the Review of Social Services in Barking and Dagenham London Borough Council* London: Audit Commission 1997

35. Audit Commission *Reviewing Social Services: guiding you through* London: Audit Commission 1999

36. Joint Reviews of Local Authorities' Social Services *A Report of the Review of Social Services in Cornwall County Council* London: Audit Commission 1998

37. Barking and Dagenham, *Op. Cit.*

38. Joint Reviews of Local Authorities' Social Services *A Report of the Review of Social Services in Coventry City Council* London: Audit Commission 1998.

39. *Clinical Governance Reviews: Judgments and Reports.* Paper presented to the meeting of the Commission for Health Improvement, 1 May 2000. Mimeo.

40. Phoebe Hall and Rudolf Klein *Caring for quality in the caring services* London: Bedford Square Press 1972

41. Audit Commission *Annual report for the year ending October 1999* London: Audit Commission 2000

42. Prime Minister and Minister for the Cabinet Office *Modernising government* London: The Stationery Office 1999 Cm 4310

43. Audit Commission *Changing picture, sharper focus: strategy 1999-2002* London: Audit Commission 1999

44. Audit Commission *Health Strategy, 2000-2003: A Consultation Document* London: Audit Commission 2000

45. Audit Commission Annual report for the year ended October 1999 *op.cit.*

46. Rudolf Klein and William Plowden *JUG meets JASP: co-ordination in government* Report of a seminar held at the Nuffield Trust, 9 March 2000. Mimeo. Also available on the Nuffield Trust web site.

47. Secretary of State for Health *The NHS Plan* London: The Stationery Office 2000 Cm 4818-1

48. Audit Commission *Health Strategy, 2000-2003 op.cit.*

49. Patricia Day and Rudolf Klein *Accountabilities* London: Tavistock 1987